Dorothy & ♡

Hale

Cassville Baptist Church Library

# The
# compassionate
# touch

# The
# compassionate
# touch

## DOUGLAS WEAD

**Creation House**
**Carol Stream, Illinois**

The royalties of this book are donated to
the work of "Saint Mark of Calcutta."

First printing—June 1977
Second printing—October 1977
Third printing—February 1978
Fourth printing—May 1978

Published by Creation House, 499 Gundersen Drive,
Carol Stream, Illinois 60187
Distributed in Canada: Beacon Distributing Ltd., 104 Consumers Drive,
Whitby, Ontario L1N 5T3
Distributed in Australia: Oracle Australia, Ltd., 18-26 Canterbury Road,
Heathmont, Victoria 135

ISBN 0-88419-015-3
Library of Congress Catalog Card No. 76-062694
Printed in the United States of America

*To my son,*
*Scott Douglas Wead*
*May he live to see a better world.*

# Author's Note

The following stories are true. Some names have been changed and events altered at the request of those involved. Conversations were reconstructed as accurately as possible. When testimony conflicted, the author made the final decision on what to include.

All accounts of street scenes and other descriptions of India are based on the observations of the author team. These observations were made prior to Mrs. Indira Ghandi's national emergency program which has dramatically improved the living conditions in India's great cities.

This book was a team effort. In addition to the author, team members included Bill Carmichael, editor of *Dayspring Magazine,* the Reverend Ken Marquis, associate pastor of Christian Center, Salem, Oregon, and the Reverend Bill Walsh, pastor of Saint Patrick's Catholic Church in Cavour, South Dakota. The team gathered information in India by tape recorded interviews and on-the-spot observation. Also each team member helped raise financial support for the project and write preliminary drafts on some of the subjects included in the book.

# *Contents*

# Introduction

Calcutta is the hellhole of the world. Hundreds of filthy streets spin uncontrollably in every direction. Open sewers run down sidewalks or back alleyways, serving as a toilet to one and a Maytag washer to another. Numerous scattered piles of dung decay wherever need for relief has come upon human or animal. Tea stalls guaranteed to give a westerner dysentery are everywhere. Smells rise and swirl around you, tormenting smells of urine and garlic, of curry powder and excrement.

Drugs abound, and though it is illegal since the Health Department will not give its stamp of approval, there is a local liquor people can afford.

Calcutta is a city of animals. Thousands of skinny pye-dogs with rabid blood roam lazily through the streets, competing with homeless children for scraps of food. Rats, which outnumber people eight to one, have become increasingly bold. In 1975 the local newspaper reported that an infant in a government hospital had been killed and eaten by rats. "The hospital will no longer admit patients without a cat," my servant at the hotel told me.

Winged life abounds. Millions of birds descend daily to devour food scraps. Mosquitoes, my least favorite form of life, are ubiquitous. Lizards eat mosquitoes, and when one appears on the wall of my hotel room, I watch helplessly, hoping it will enjoy its new environment and stay a long time. Unfortunately there are few lizards in Calcutta.

The most famous creature is still the sacred cow. There are not as many here as in other great cities of India, but they are still a curious attraction. They wander unmolested in the very center of traffic.

Mostly, Calcutta is people—all kinds of people, eight million of them. People with hollow eyes and consumptive coughs. People in

9

rags with broken and twisted limbs. Hideous, toothless hags out of a Grimm's fairy tale and mini-skirted prostitutes, probably the youngest in the world. There are heavily loaded ricksha drivers running down the streets at a five-mile-an-hour clip. They should have huge muscular legs and bulging biceps; instead, they are slender-legged and tired, since there is not enough to eat in this city. They throw ugly scowls at the people who walk by.

Some people, however, get plenty to eat. These are the beautiful women in colorful saris and handsome young men with mustaches and western shoes. On Park Street, you may sometimes see suits. They are usually wrinkled and shiny, but if you stay long enough, you may glimpse a polyester sport coat. There are business men in Calcutta—some are even millionaires.

Then, there are the university students. They have an excellent education and are well read. They would curse these paragraphs, but they will leave Calcutta by the thousands to work as doctors or psychiatrists in the West.

You could discover a kind of middle-class community in Calcutta —the wage earners. Because of constant inflation, it is hard to state their earning power in terms of American dollars, but at this writing, a factory worker can count on seventy-eight cents a day. Sometimes he will earn more, sometimes less. Since the oil cartel, things are increasingly expensive. A Coca Cola may cost a half-day's pay. But the factory worker is still in luck. He has a steady income.

Thousands of others in this middle class awaken each morning with only their wits. They take one day at a time, scrounging for work wherever they can. A coolie's job pays poorly, only thirty-nine cents a day, but thousands of young people must work all week for the equivalent of one American dollar. Still, a person with any work at all seems lucky in contrast to The Poor.

In the bustees, the sprawling slums of Calcutta, live the poorest people on earth. There are thousands of them. No cars can reach the back roads, and a visitor with a camera would be lucky to get in, much less get out. Many of these people are fiercely proud. They live in huts built as temporary dwellings. Instead of staying days, they have stayed years.

Some know they are poor. They are in no mood to have visitors. But most are ignorant of how poor they are. They have known no other life.

10

The old Indian aristocracy is right. Many of them are happy. The children play cricket in narrow alleyways. They laugh at jokes. Their parents give the pleasant sighs of love at night, and people feel better after they have slept. This does not mean they do not wish to be rid of the rats that eat their food and the lice that breed in their hair. They know about malnutrition, would like clean skin without running sores, and wish their teeth did not rot so quickly. They are conscious that something is wrong—too many are dying, especially the children. Those who are happy, are happy in spite of their poverty, not because of it.

There are stories in these bustees, thousands of horrible stories. Stories of orphans who, reaching the awkward age when they no longer incite pity in their neighbors, cannot count on help. Overwhelmed by hunger or disease, they wander, dazed, through the last weeks of their lives. They are too weak to struggle, yet too tough to die easily. They cry for help, but there are too many of them. No one can hear them anyway.

There are stories of parents who sell their children or force their daughters into prostitution, and of thieves who will steal a man's only blanket for one more glass of liquor.

But there are good stories in Calcutta, too—even in the bustees —stories of tough people who will die before they will hurt or cheat anyone, of heroic, visionary government officials who cannot be compromised, and stories of the famous and lovely Mother Teresa. These are small lights in a morass of darkness and corruption. They are small, but they are not insignificant.

This book is about one of those lights from Calcutta. A mysterious and provocative man, he has appeared out of nowhere, a phantom angel to thousands of homeless children and crippled beggars. He feeds them like a lover of nature would feed hungry birds. He sets their crippled wings, and when they are able, lets them fly freely away. Yet always they return to him.

He is a white man, which makes his story all the more unlikely. He is fiercely pro-government, lecturing the West on the advance of India since her independence.

I heard his beautiful, paradoxical story from successful men in suits who came out of bustees. I heard it from crippled children who now can walk. I heard it a hundred times, and it will haunt me for the rest of my life.

11

*Raju*

# 1

Asha lives in a Calcutta bustee. You cannot imagine anyone as poor as Asha. Her few pots and rags could be demanded at any moment by any of a half-dozen people who have helped her. When she became pregnant, her husband left. For eleven years she has lived with her crippled son at the doorstep of a one-room shack.

Asha knows her home well. She has memorized every curve of the ground. Each rain reshapes her home rather like rearranging one's bedroom furniture. It also rains on Asha and her son, for they do not live in the shack—they live on the doorstep.

A Muslim man lives inside with his wife and large family. He generously offers his doorstep in exchange for Asha's body. Asha's relationship with the man's wife is understandably strained. Raju, Asha's son, was kicked around all of his life and sometimes beaten unmercifully until one day when he was discovered by a strange and powerful man.

On that day, as on all the days before it, Raju had worked his way to a nearby main street. It was not a main street in the way that you or I would picture a main street, but it was made of large stones, and occasionally a car or truck passed. It was crowded with pedestrians and bicyclists, important-looking people who were hurrying to places of work, carrying large sacks on their heads, or pushing old wooden carts filled with garbage. At the tea stalls on this street, he could overhear conversation and sometimes learn about places far beyond walking distance. I should say crawling distance, because Raju is crippled.

Why Raju liked to visit this street is hard to say. Perhaps he liked the anonymity, or perhaps his tormentors could not find him here. But whatever his reasons, Raju crawled like a spider every day through the filthy alleys, carefully avoiding the dysentery stools and little puddles of urine.

15

One day a beautiful cream-colored automobile appeared. It cut through the crowds like the bow of a ship parting the ocean. He had heard its horn honking; so by the time it passed, he was in a good position to view it.

Suddenly the car screeched to a stop. A white sahib emerged and stared intently toward him. The little boy sat, frozen by the stranger's stare as an animal freezes when it looks into automobile headlights. Breaking the spell, he hurriedly crawled away. The sahib pursued, gaining rapidly, until suddenly Raju felt himself jerked up into the air by his ragged clothes. His heart leaped and his eyes grew terrified. He had never known such fear.

A crowd assembled quickly around the sahib who, with his wire glasses and slick hair, looked as though he had stepped right out of the 1950s. They stared at his watch, his shoes, his teeth; but he seemed strangely unaware of the angry emotions around him. This lack of fear neutralized the young Muslims who circled the crowd, staring at him and cursing softly.

The sahib could see no one but Raju. He saw an eleven year old, with legs only three quarters of an inch in diameter, about the size of a broom handle. They were curved and twisted, and since Raju could not stand, he hung from the sahib's grip, his bruised face filled with fear.

The neighborhood must have been amused by all of this sudden interest in a little person who for years had crept around their alleys like a crab among the rocks.

"Where are the parents of this boy?" the sahib shouted.

They all may have despised the white man, but there was an immediate contest to escort him to Asha. Men like this had been known to drop rupees for such meaningless information. The sahib left his car in the middle of the street and followed the small delegation through the twisted alleyways to the Muslim man's doorstep.

Asha was there. A neighbor emerged from the adjacent mud hut and squatted next to her.

"Are you this boy's parents?"

They stared back suspiciously.

"I want to take this boy to the hospital." He waited for some sign that they understood. They were all silent. "I will feed him and have a doctor operate on him. Please."

The white man turned to the crowd to see if any face sympathized with him. "Don't you want me to help this boy? He is going to die. He needs food and medicine. He can be taught how to walk. I don't want any money. It will all be free."

Asha's mouth gaped open stupidly. She wanted to reach out and grab the man before he disappeared, but her hand would not move.

"No," the neighbor shouted. He couldn't figure out this white man's game. The Muslim man should come home to make such a decision.

"Jesus wants to help this boy," the sahib said. Even after twenty years in India, he still used the same religious jargon. In the West he would be laughed off the streets; in India it didn't seem to matter. He was often lonely here, and it helped him speak freely.

The people only stared, completely mystified. He turned to Asha. "I will take him to the hospital. You can come and see him every day. He needs food, and he needs an operation."

"It is not free," the neighbor man shouted.

Now the sahib understood. "Oh. Yes, it is free, absolutely free. I will not let you pay anything. It is free," he nodded, and several in the crowd began to nod with him.

The neighbor man smiled and put his hand on Asha's shoulder. "It is free, Asha."

Asha was beside herself, overjoyed and hysterical at once.

The sahib squatted next to Asha and reverently closed his eyes while all around him stared dumbfounded. "Oh, God, have mercy on this little family. Let this boy live. Guide the surgeon's hands and heal this boy. Let him walk back here and show all these lovely people that you care for them."

The crowd watched, some perplexed, others giggling. Someone kept asking him, "Is it free? Is it free?"

"Yes, yes," he would answer.

They all broke into laughter. They laughed for different happy reasons. They laughed so hard their reasons ran together.

Lifting Raju in his arms, the white man motioned to Asha. "Come with us. Let me show you our hospital."

They returned to the automobile and the crowd scattered in a downpour as the automobile sped away. Along the main street people

17

were scrambling for cover. Street vendors had packed their cartons of cigarettes and pulled back under the shelter of the roofs and porches.

Even with the windshield wipers thrashing violently, the white man couldn't see; so he stopped the automobile and sat nervously tapping his fingers on the steering wheel.

"Look at the people," he sighed "There are thousands and thousands of people. We will build a big hospital some day." He turned to Asha. "Our present facility is very, very small."

Asha smiled. "Free?" she asked.

"Yes, yes, free," he answered and turned back to the street to watch the people.

Suddenly he opened his door and raced down the street. An Indian, wearing a dark suit, stood in the rain.

"Sir?" the white man called out.

The stunned Indian set his briefcase down. "Are you speaking to me?"

"Yes, sir. You mustn't stand in the rain like this. You're a gentleman. Come, I'll give you a ride."

The Indian smiled, a little surprised and pleased that the white man had spotted him. "Oh, that's quite all right, I'm waiting for a taxi."

Though he was a stubborn fellow, the white man managed to persuade him. Soaked, they plopped into the front seat, laughing heartily.

"This is Raju!" the white man said triumphantly.

The automobile was stuffy now. The old woman stank, and the white man's wet clothes smelled, too. The Indian gentleman was upset by the skeleton lying in the back seat, but he smiled nervously.

"What are you going to do with him?"

The white man drove slowly away. "I am going to take him to my hospital. This is his mother, Asha."

The woman smiled sheepishly and rearranged her rags as though for protection.

"How will they pay?"

"Oh, it will be free. I will pay for it myself somehow." He glanced into the rear view mirror at the woman. "Free," he said to her in Bengali.

She nodded her head and smiled widely. "Thank you, thank you. Yes, free. Free. Thank you. Thank you."

"Wonderful," the Indian gentleman said. "Astonishing. You are a doctor?"

"Oh, no. I am the pastor of a church on Royd Street."

"And you are here to convert us all to Christianity?"

The white man hesitated. "We are involved in a lot of work. Dozens and dozens of people are helping us. We have a large school and a food program and a hospital. . . . "

"Oh, you have a hospital?"

"A very small one. Only sixteen beds. But someday we shall build a very, very large hospital. One with a hundred beds!"

"That will take millions of dollars."

"It will take a miracle, but it will happen."

The Indian gentleman glanced into the back seat. He stared at Raju and the old woman. "So you will take him to your hospital?"

"Oh, we will save him," the white man answered, reading the gentleman's thoughts. "He will live. Ones worse than him live. I wouldn't be surprised if he can be taught to walk. Of course, it will require several operations."

"Astonishing." *He is a strange one, this priest,* the Indian gentleman thought. *He is like a Mother Teresa.*

It began to rain again. Raindrops clung to the automobile windows like clusters of diamonds. Raju stared in fascination, not comprehending all that was happening around him.

The white man smiled, his heart filled with the prospect of saving a life. He felt slightly ashamed for interrupting such a noble mission to pick up the stranger in the rain.

The Indian gentleman seemed to sense this. "You should not have stopped for me," he said with embarrassment.

"Oh no, no," the white man recovered. "I could not let you stand in the rain."

It would be many months before he learned that stopping for the Indian gentleman was the most important good deed of his twenty-two years in Calcutta.

One day the birds circling high above the Christian Mission Hospital were witness to a beautiful moment. Several Indian nurses gathered in the courtyard. Dr. Chatterjee was there. His face was wrinkled and tired, but he stood straight and dignified. Marie John was there. She had worked patiently for months to witness this.

Raju stood precariously on his feet, without help. A few yards away the sahib waited, shifting anxiously from one foot to the next. "Thank you, God. Oh, Jesus, thank you for this day."

Raju walked five yards and fell into the arms of the sahib. The nurses cheered. The old doctor smiled. The sahib cried. And Raju, his head buried in the white man's stomach, was crying, too. Even though he cried tears of joy, the white man must not see.

"He always brags about my smile. I love the pastor. He has saved my life. I am a Christian. I always smile."

The telephone was ringing; a secretary shouted for the pastor. He could have broken the boy's tiny grip easily, but it was more important to linger here a moment. Raju rubbed his face in the white man's stomach and pulled away, flashing his white teeth.

"That Raju," the pastor said loudly to someone nearby. "He's always smiling."

Raju still lives in a Muslim bustee. He awakens each morning and walks to the Mahatma Ghandi School on the mission compound. He sheds his rags, showers and puts on a clean uniform. He studies hard all day.

In the afternoon, he waits with other children by the pastor's door. Eventually the sahib emerges and spots Raju. He hugs him tightly. "I love you," he always says, "and Jesus loves you even more."

After this Raju rushes off. He changes back into his dirty clothes and boards a bus that drops him off near his bustee. At night he sleeps with his mother on the Muslim man's doorstep. He dreams of waking in the morning. He dreams of a wonderful shower and a delicious noon meal, his only food for the day. He will wait again all afternoon for the sahib to say, "I love you."

When he dies? "When I die I will go to heaven," Raju says, with a very serious look on his face. "You see, God loves me very, very much."

*Lorissa*

# 2

There was not much known about Lorissa's mother except that she was a prostitute. She could not afford to have a daughter, so her baby was fed into that great stream of Calcutta orphans.

If Lorissa could survive infancy, she had a good chance of living to be five or six years old. The little children of the street strike such a pitiful note there is usually someone on the block who will help.

From six until the adolescent years the odds against life are high again. Not only childhood disease but the awkwardness of their age is against survival. The child is too little for useful labor, or even prostitution, and yet too big to attract attention or pity. There are many other smaller children on the streets. The competition is great.

Some children are lucky enough to find a family willing to take care of them. But they will be "extras," and when the budget is cut or food is low, the orphan will be the one fed last. Understandably so; the others are working and they are bound by blood.

The ones who are not so lucky die. No one knows how many there are. Sometimes they have no name, but are simply referred to as "the one with measles," or "smallpox," or "diptheria," or more commonly, "dysentery." Any disease can kill a child who has no strength or resistance to fight it off.

Some starve to death, not very many to be sure, because it is a strong child who can live to starve to death. He must survive every conceivable bacterial and viral attack with a body too weak to resist. His vital organs are usually damaged, and death may be caused by some malfunction of the heart. His teeth are rotten, his stomach bloated, and he will have bald spots on his head. These dead lie with a puzzled look on their faces while some adult, a handkerchief gripped to nose and mouth, determines what happened. Eventually they become a statistic in an *Information Please Almanac* that sits on a grocery store shelf somewhere in the United States.

Lorissa was very lucky. She was given to the celebrated Catholic sister, Mother Teresa. Her mother made the presentation one day and never returned, probably satisfied that her daughter had a better start in life than her own. Though many children move through that Catholic institution and Lorissa was adopted when she was one year old, she is remembered. "She had the biggest brown eyes. We hated to lose her." If Lorissa was lost to the Sisters of Charity, she was indeed found by George Johnathan Chandler.

Chandler was a black who had fled the New York ghettos as a teenager and sailed the oceans of the world as a merchant marine. He was tough, wise and experienced. Having overcome the bitterness of younger years, he had learned to enjoy people and to enjoy living. But he was saddened by the fact that he was now too old to put his knowledge of life to work. Then life gave George a second chance.

It was very unlikely that Chandler would find someone to love in Calcutta, but he did. Trudi was a middle-aged anglo-Indian. She, too, had given up most of her dreams. Theirs was a torrid romance, each living to the fullest moments they had concluded would never come. Their love apparently overcame the staggering cultural differences, and the Chandlers were married.

Too old to have a child of their own, they adopted Lorissa. Life had even granted them that. She was the supreme token of their love. The Chandlers were grateful.

That first night, George Jonathan Chandler sat by his new daughter's cot and wept with joy. "Some day we are going to America," he announced the next morning. "It is a country of unbelievable wealth." George said that knowing that if they lived in America it would be in a New York slum, crowded with drugs and fear. But Harlem even at its worst, would come as a pleasant surprise to his little family after life in Calcutta.

"I will go first," he explained to his wife. "There will be some legal work, and I must get a job."

Trudi openly applauded the idea though secretly she feared it. Life in America was difficult to comprehend. She was confused by her husband's descriptions and preferred to ignore the subject. George Chandler's plans developed while his wife refused to believe they would ever happen. But two years after they adopted Lorissa, Chandler left for the United States. It was a tearful farewell with many em-

23

braces. George could sense the fear and desperation in his wife.

"Be brave," he smiled, "this will work perfectly. I would never take a chance that might lose my two girls. We will meet in New York."

Trudi watched the taxi disappear down the crowded street. He was a wise man; she knew that. He was a very strong man and had survived many difficult years. His plan was probably a very good one, but she was afraid she would never see him again. She stood and cried, looking down the street at the spot where the taxi had vanished. *He is less than a mile from me now, but within an hour he may be gone forever.*

Mrs. Chandler was right, her husband did not return. A cablegram came instead.

For more than a month she tried to handle her problems alone. Finally the pressures became too great. She was told there was a man on Royd Street who could help her, and one afternoon she went to the mission compound. She was told to wait. "The pastor is very busy," they said. "Can you come back tomorrow?"

Trudi returned the next day; she waited for hours in the courtyard. The sun shone brilliantly making mockery of her depression. The white man emerged from his office. The children instantly gathered around him. They were laughing and they were happy.

*Of course they are happy,* Trudi thought. *Their lives have been touched by God. Or is it God?* She wondered. *Maybe it is just the white man who has chosen them. Who is he to decide that Lorissa should not be helped? I am not a beggar,* she thought. *I have never asked anyone for help.* For a moment, she considered rushing the man and insisting on an interview, but her anger and her pride restrained her.

"Mrs. Chandler?" A young Indian teenager timidly approached her.

"Yes."

"Follow me."

"Why will they not let me see the pastor?" she said angrily.

"Oh, you can see the pastor," the teenager smiled. "You must understand this is an extremely busy week. But believe me, it is much better for you to see his wife." The teenager smiled broadly and then added with a whisper, "She is the brains. You should see her."

The memsahib was seated at a desk in a large room. There were other desks in the room; they seemed to cover the floor like wall to wall carpeting. Each desk was a beehive of activity.

"Mrs. Chandler?" The white woman stood and extended her hand. She too was a legend in this neighborhood, though she was not dramatic in her work. She did not wear old clothes; she was probably more contemporary in her grooming than many of the western visitors who passed through the mission each year. Her clothes could have been taken from the backs of *Vogue* magazine's latest models. But the white woman's appearance was deceptive, for beneath her smart clothes was a fierce devotion to India—her people, her suffering, and her exotic and colorful history. Behind her fashionable appearance was a sharp mind of great organizational ability. The young worker on Royd Street spoke the truth when he whispered to his visitor, "She is the brains of this place."

Trudi was nervously aware, as stacks of paper moved from desk to desk, that this was a busy place. She would have to hurry. "Can you help me? I am a Christian."

"Now, Mrs. Chandler, just take your time and tell me what has happened."

"I have lost my husband," Trudi paused. She said no more. She maintained her composure, but it was apparent that she was near the breaking point. "Here is a cablegram." She passed the paper across the desk. It was folded and worn, though only a month old.

The white woman read the yellow paper. "Your husband was an American citizen?"

"Yes," the anglo-Indian's face was sweating now. She wiped her forehead with a rag.

"Have you spoken to someone at the American Consulate?"

"Yes, yes, I spent a whole day there. They said that they are not responsible for me or my child."

"Now, what is your problem?" The white woman was tender. "You have no money?"

Trudi nodded, slowly. "He was a good man and he sent us money from the United States. Then one day I received this cablegram from his sister saying he died of a cerebral hemorrhage. There was no warning. Just like that, he died."

"Do you have work?"

Mrs. Chandler swallowed hard. "Yes, I help my landlady. She is a

25

Moslem. There is not enough money. When we adopted Lorissa, George had income, too. But they pay me very little. Mine alone is not enough."

"Do you have food?"

"No, memsahib." Then the Indian woman began to sob. Her efforts to hold it back prompted a coughing spell which made more noise and drew more attention than her tears. Mrs. Chandler sat in her chair and wept in shame.

The white woman leaned across the desk and patted Mrs. Chandler's hand. "Now, dear, you just go ahead and cry." She spoke to someone nearby, then turned back to the anglo-Indian. "Mrs. Chandler, is Lorissa with you?"

"Yes, I take her everywhere," the anglo-Indian woman said. She was slowly recovering from her sudden outburst. She shifted in her seat and lowered her voice to a whisper. "Of course, I have to give as much food as I can to Lorissa. I have been very weak, memsahib." The Indian woman was clearly ashamed to have to admit this. "The landlord says she will not keep me. I am a Christian. My father was a Catholic. Did I say that?"

The white woman smiled, "That doesn't matter. We will do whatever we can. Would you please have your daughter come in?"

When Mrs. Chandler returned with Lorissa, the white woman was involved in an exchange with two ladies at her desk. She abruptly halted her conversation and smiled at the little girl. "This is Lorissa? Come here, Lorissa," the white woman said. The little Indian girl timidly approached the desk. "Would you like to come to our school?"

Lorissa put her fingers in her mouth and slowly shook her head. The memsahib laughed. "There are many children here. You would play and have a lot of fun. Are you sure?" Lorissa only stared at the white woman. "You would just go to the school in the daytime. In the nighttime you would go home to Mommy."

"We'll take her," the white woman said. "But you are going to have to see one of our doctors, Mrs. Chandler." She handed a note to the Indian teenager standing nearby. "Could you do that right now?"

The Indian teenager left the office with Mrs. Chandler right behind. When they returned, Lorissa was in the courtyard. The white woman was taking a rare moment away from her paper work; she stood in the afternoon sunshine watching Lorissa kicking an empty box. Lorissa giggled delightedly, looking back at the memsahib for approval.

"Lorissa and I will be good friends," the white woman said. She paused a moment to read a note handed her by the teenager. "Mrs. Chandler," she said, "you have a very serious heart condition. I'm afraid you are going to have to go to the hospital."

"Oh no, I can't do that. I have to work."

"You have no real choice, Mrs. Chandler. Your condition is very serious. We can get one of the ladies in our church to take care of Lorissa."

"Oh, memsahib, I could never leave Lorissa."

"You go home and think about it. No one can make you go to the hospital, Mrs. Chandler, but your condition is very serious."

"I have to work, memsahib."

"We will help make arrangements for you. Our hospital doesn't have the facilities you will need, but we will help arrange it."

"No, no, memsahib. I can't. I can't!"

The white woman put her arm around Lorissa's mother. "Now, don't you worry about it today. You think about it tomorrow. Nobody can make you do anything. We just want to help you. Lorissa needs you. You are going to have to take care of yourself."

"Yes, memsahib, thank you. Lorissa will be a good student. Your teachers will like her. I will be very careful; please don't worry about me."

The white woman watched Mrs. Chandler leave with her daughter. She turned to the teenager nearby. "That woman should be in a hospital right now."

The teenager followed Mrs. Chandler with his eyes. "What can we do?"

The white woman put her hands on her hips and sighed deeply, "Not a thing."

# 3

The memsahib sat at her desk. She was very busy. The percussion of adding machines rattled in the background. Out of the corner of her eyes, she could see someone standing near the door. She feared it was someone who wanted her. She was too involved to interrupt her work now, so ignored the movement hoping whoever it was would note her concentration and return later. The shapes came forward anyway, and she turned as two Moslem women approached. Standing behind them was a little four-year-old girl.

"This girl's mother died last night," one of the ladies said loudly.

The white woman was somewhat taken aback by their forwardness. Several heads in the room turned toward the scene. She glanced at the little girl by the door. It was Lorissa. She was twirling her fingers in her dress and mumbling something happy. *Oh, God, it is so wise of you to keep tragedy beyond the understanding of children,* she thought.

"We can't take this child," one of the Moslem women said. "We have lots of work. We have lost a week's rent already."

The other woman spoke quickly, almost apologetically, as though to ease the hard words of her friend. "You must understand how difficult it has been. Mrs. Chandler has been so sick she could not work. She has been a terrible burden, and we have lost much rent money."

"How did Mrs. Chandler die?" The white woman finally asked.

"I don't know!" The first lady answered defiantly, as though resenting a cross-examination, though the white woman was only curious.

"We stayed up with her all night," the second woman said softly. "I didn't think it right for Lorissa to be alone with her mother's body."

"And where is the body now," the white woman growled, standing to her feet, shocked that the women would keep Lorissa all night with her mother's corpse. Even if they cared nothing for the little girl, their religious views would seem to prohibit this.

"It is still in the room, and it must be out right away!" The first lady shouted back.

"Well, ladies, you have been very considerate," the white woman said sarcastically, controlling her anger.

"What about that little girl?" the first lady asked. "You are responsible; she goes to your school. She has nothing to do with us."

Several workers in the room lifted their eyes from typewriters and adding machines to share mischievous looks. They had seen the righteous wrath of the white woman and watched in amused anticipation as the two Moslem women ignorantly walked into a confrontation they would probably lose.

The memsahib bit her lip and looked across the room. The workers quickly feigned disinterest, returning to their adding machines and typewriters as though not even aware of the conversation. Lorissa remained completely oblivious, waiting patiently and humming to herself.

"If you want Lorissa's things, we will bring them to you tomorrow," the second lady murmured.

"Before she died, Lorissa's mother told us to keep all of her things," the first woman stated aggressively.

The memsahib looked at the woman sternly. "You leave her room alone!"

"She owes us rent."

"You leave the room alone. Don't you touch a single thing." The Moslem woman caught the fury in the memsahib's voice and said nothing.

Suddenly Lorissa came racing across the room, flung herself into the memsahib's arms, and broke into sobs. Gasping for air, she tried to speak, but no words came. She could not seem to capture enough air for more than pitiful sounds and cries of frustration. She seemed afraid that if she did not say something quickly, her audience would be gone forever, but try as she would, she could only whimper and stutter, "I . . . I . . . I." Her grip on the white woman tightened until her knuckles were white.

29

The memsahib held Lorissa firmly. She did not want to turn her back on the Moslem women, for then Lorissa would have to face them over her shoulder. Instead, she just closed her eyes. "Now, honey, we love you," she said. "Lorissa, listen to me darling. Don't cry; we love you."

Stuttering and gasping for breath, Lorissa said slowly, between sobs, "I . . . I . . . I don't have a Mommy or Daddy anymore."

The memsahib glared her dismissal at the two ladies. "Don't you touch a thing in that room!" she repeated and stalked out of the office with Lorissa clinging tightly.

Lorissa would not loosen her grip as they sat together in the courtyard. Her tears now soaked the white woman's shoulder.

"Lorissa?" the memsahib whispered. "Lorissa?" But the little girl could not stop the convulsions. *I thought she did not know what had happened. Oh, God, how this breaks Your heart.* "Lorissa," she said again. This time the little girl's sobs finally came to an end. She was breathing deeply, and the white woman knew that at last the orphan could hear her. "Lorissa, I am your new Mommy," she said deliberately. "You are coming home to live with me."

Lorissa said nothing, but clung tightly until the white woman's neck and arms began to ache. They sat for a long time. The memsahib ran her fingers through Lorissa's black hair and smiled to herself. *Well, God, what do you know? I am a mother again.* She buried her head in the little girl's black hair and wept for joy. She knew that she already loved the orphan, and she knew that Lorissa would bring much excitement and much sorrow to the apartment where she lived.

For the rest of the afternoon and long into the evening, Lorissa played in the courtyard. The white woman glanced up from her desk from time to time. Lorissa appeared happy, as though the morning of tears had not happened. This time the memsahib was not fooled. She knew what emotions were running just beneath the surface of the little girl.

At dark, when the pastor eventually left his office, the woman went to meet him. "Come with me, Lorissa," she said, taking her hand. When she opened the door to the automobile and motioned, Lorissa scooted into the front seat next to the pastor. "This is your new Daddy, Lorissa." The sahib shot a quick glance at his wife. She met it steadily. He turned to Lorissa.

"Hello," the white man said, and he hugged the little girl. He was content to wait for an explanation when they got home.

The memsahib lifted her onto her own lap and moved next to her husband. "Isn't she a pretty little girl?"

"I believe she is the prettiest little girl in the world," the pastor declared.

The ride to the white man's apartment was long and exciting. Lorissa was wide-eyed at the street scenes which looked so different from the automobile. She wanted to stand up to look out the front window but was much too shy to do so. They turned onto a main street which was no longer crowded with people. Soon they were traveling faster than Lorissa had ever traveled before, even on her occasional trolley ride.

She was filled with wonder to hear that her new home would be much larger than two rooms. Lorissa's long exciting ride was really only a matter of blocks.

The sahib parked his car and rushed to a nearby door calling, "We have to be back in an hour." Lorissa looked up at the tall, three-story apartment. "Do we live here?" The pastor's wife laughed. "Our apartment is on the third floor. I am afraid we have quite a walk."

The sahib stood just inside the door, talking to an Indian man nearby. "Lorissa," the white man picked the little girl up in his arms. "I want you to meet Kumar. He has leprosy. But we love him, and he lives with us here."

Lorissa could see the pots and stained rags spread out under the stairway. "He sleeps right over there," the white man pointed. "Since he is sick, we cannot touch his things or play with him. Okay?"

The leper smiled and nodded approval. Lorissa turned away and hugged the white man's neck. The pastor began the long climb up the stairs.

"Do you know what leprosy is?" the white woman asked. She was walking up the stairs just behind them. Lorissa nodded. "He is a very lonely man. His wife and children love him, but they cannot go near him. You mustn't go near him either, but you may smile and be friendly to him. We will feed him and take care of him."

When they reached a landing, he sat the little girl down, puffing heavily from his long climb. A young Indian boy came bounding down the stairs chasing a loose ball. An old man lay on a cot nearby;

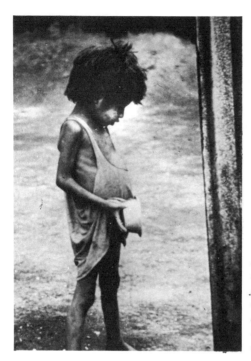

*Street orphan waits at the mission for the ration of food which keeps him alive. The mission has served more than a million meals during its existence.*

*This is home for one poverty-stricken family in Calcutta.*

he mumbled angrily at the noise. At the top of the stairs there were more children. A thirteen-year-old Indian was helping a four year old take off a western T-shirt. Lorissa stared curiously at the children and then followed the pastor through a door.

An old Indian greeted him, shaking his finger angrily, "If you don't get those boys to bring up the water, we will not have supper tonight."

A young Indian teenager stepped into the room from an adjacent door. "We have running water!" he shouted mischievously. "The water in the bathtub is already almost half an inch deep in some places."

"You get downstairs and bring me up some water," the old man shouted angrily. The boy disappeared.

Ignoring them both, the sahib carried Lorissa through the apartment, introduced her to more than fifteen persons who made up the family, and took her into a nearby room where cots lined the wall. The white woman was unfolding a blanket.

The young boy reappeared, "Is our new sister going to sleep in my room?"

"Yes," the white woman said. "Is that all right?"

"Oh, we will all be glad to have her in here." He turned to the sahib, changing the subject as if bringing home a new sister were an everyday occurrence.

"The water is really working better, you know."

"Do you have it on full?" the pastor asked.

"Yes."

"How long has it been running?"

"I turned it on before we retired last night."

"And it is only half an inch deep?"

The boy nodded.

The sahib shook his head. "That is not enough to make any difference."

"How much water do you want?" the boy asked in frustration.

"It should work just as well as the waterspout outside."

"But how can you expect to get that pressure way up here?"

The white man looked at him in amazement. "That makes no difference. Many of the large apartment buildings on this street have sufficient water pressure. It doesn't matter what floor you are on."

The boy just turned and walked out. The white man heard the old

Indian shouting at him in the other room. The sahib smiled. He had lived for twenty-two years without running water; it didn't make much difference to him now.

Word of the new arrival spread through the apartment. Members of the white man's great family looked into the small room. There were many other children and teenagers, and old men and women. They would peer around the corner of the door, look at Lorissa, smile and nod politely, then return to their work.

"Mommy and Daddy live in there," the white woman said. She pointed to an open doorway through which a large double bed could be seen. "Lorissa sleeps here." She patted one of the little cots lining the wall. "Mommy and Daddy sleep in there."

The white man took his wife's hand. "Lorissa, go to the kitchen and tell Batu that you want something to eat." He pointed, smiled and shut the door to the bedroom firmly. "Now, Huldah, tell me what have you done?"

"Her mother died last night, right while she was playing in the room. She has no one in the world to help her now. And the landlord threw her out."

The apartment was already full of people now. Every room and every corner was taken. It had always been that way. It was as if the mission, and the school, and the food program, and the little hospital were not enough. They took their work home with them. Their apartment had become just another of the sixty centers they had begun in West Bengal.

The white man collapsed into a chair. He was pleased, though he decided not to show it immediately. It was usually he who brought home the old men, and women, and children. One night they'd had quite a talk about it and his wife's wisdom had prevailed. They could not hope to help very many people in their small apartment. They should have privacy and rest. They should save themselves for the masses of orphans, drug addicts and beggars whose problems constantly drained them. They had a tough schedule, rising at four in the morning and returning for supper at eight; their few hours at home should be special. So they had said. But she was the one who had broken their secret promise.

The white man pulled her onto his lap. He was laughing.

"What's so funny?" she said with a pout. She suspected what he was thinking, but tried to seem innocently indignant. "I said, what's so funny!" But her husband's laughter was infectious. Soon they were both laughing.

They were like two overweight lovers, who had sworn themselves to a strict diet. One of them had just ordered a banana split, and the other one was asking for an extra spoon. They were laughing at themselves, at their weakness for the poor people around them, and at their broken promise.

The door opened. A wrinkled old man entered, bowing slightly. His face was flushed, and in spite of his great respect for the sahib, he was giggling uncontrollably at the sight of the couple together in the small chair. Lorissa stood at his side in tears, overcome by the strange people and surroundings.

"Ohhhh, Lorissa," the white woman exclaimed, jumping from the chair, but the sahib responded quickly too, and in a twinkling had swung the little girl up into the air. She landed, bouncing, on the bed, a confused expression on her face as she decided whether to be terrified or to enjoy the bounce. The white man tossed her again. By this time she had decided to enjoy it and laughed with the tears still on her cheeks.

"Now, now. We won't have jumping on the bed," the white woman said properly, but with a twinkle. As she led her out of the bedroom, Lorissa looked back at the white man, who defiantly bounced himself lightly on the bed. The wrinkled old man was still giggling his shrill little laugh. He bowed several times before shutting the door.

"Yes, sahib. Yes, sahib," he kept repeating with embarrassment, even though the white man had not said anything to him.

The sahib lay back on the bed exhausted. His wife walking little Lorissa out of the bedroom brought back memories. He thought of Bonnie, their only child by birth. He thought of America and the college in which she was enrolled. He wondered where she was at that very moment. He would soon love Lorissa just as he loved Bonnie. It seemed impossible, yet he knew it would happen.

He thought of the thousands of other homeless children, of Eikash and Sinjeet, two street orphans he had met that day on Royd Street. He could not bring them all home. There was not enough room nor enough love in any one home to touch them all. He lay on the bed and looked into the face of God. There was nothing to say.

*Bimal*

# 4

A visit to a Calcutta train station is a visit to hell. Beggars swarm along the steps like mosquitoes hungry for blood, but it isn't blood they want, only coins. They know you have coins or you could not ride the train.

It is fatal to drop a coin into a tin cup: it crashes, resounding like a giant hammer against a bell, and attracts a hundred more beggars in an instant. Not the same sensation as watching sea gulls gather for bread, more like lifting the lid to a garbage can and being overwhelmed by swarms of tiny gnats.

At nighttime it is worse. Desperation is on the prowl. Policemen cannot see everything, and low-watt light bulbs give off a very pale yellow glow. The corridors are filled with refugees; the floors crawl with bodies, some moaning, some quiet. There is an eerie feeling that the station is itself some grotesque monster with hundreds of arms and eyes. If it is a monster, it is terribly sick, spitting and coughing its poisonous breath into the narrow halls.

To an Indian the train station is not hell. It is a public service, once the exclusive property of the rich, now part of the glory of the new India. Millions can now afford to ride these trains. It is only the narrow-minded, spoiled westerner who looks about him and gasps as though entering Dachau.

Bimal had always loved the Calcutta train station, the shouting and pushing, the last minute fear that he might be on the wrong platform, the exciting shrill whistle of the train.

He had seen the hungry eyes. They had told him his life was better; he could be proud of his work. Sometimes Bimal had despised the poor refugees. The gods must be angry with them or they would not be allowed to suffer.

This day was different. Today Bimal did not despise the refugees, nor did he pity them. He would gladly trade places with the men who lay sick in the dark corridors of the train station. He would gladly lay his small reed mat on the floor and call it home. At least they had freedom to move about. At least they had hope.

Bimal was led through the crowded hall by his sahib friend. The Indian looked like a zombie. For all practical purposes he was, because he was going to Purulia. Only an Indian can tell you why going to Purulia is worse than dying alone in a crowded depot.

The white man was very much alive. He was rushing to the ticket counter and arranging for the baggage. He was pulling and leading Bimal through the corridors. He was checking his watch and rereading his ticket. He was running down the platform and talking to station employees. Often he would return to Bimal, look into his eyes, and chat with him as though Bimal were some very precious cargo that the sahib would die for. He was.

When the train pulled up, the sahib found a first class compartment. He placed their luggage in the racks, and the men sat opposite each other on benches which would double as their beds.

The white man tried the light switch. It didn't work. He took a piece of cardboard from the floor and began pushing the trash out of the compartment. He was always trying to improve things, this white man. When the room was cleared, he used some discarded rags to dry the floor, wet with urine and rain.

Bimal sat quietly watching.

The train began to pull out of the station. Both men moved to the windows. They sat in silence, catching glimpses of the city. Soon Calcutta disappeared into the darkness.

Bimal glanced suspiciously at the white man. Could he read his thoughts? Did he know he planned to commit suicide? A jump from the speeding train would be much quicker and less painful for everyone involved. No one really cared anyway. Bimal had learned that these last few days. No one except the sahib. *Yes, the sahib cares,* Bimal concluded. *That is why I must wait until he sleeps.*

Neither man spoke. They each respected the silence of the other. The monotonous clicking rhythm of the steel wheels on the track was a tranquilizer no one could resist. Bimal, with all his fears and frustrations, found himself drifting to sleep. He was more relaxed now; with the train moving, he knew the peace of death was only a few steps away—as soon as the sahib went to sleep.

It must have been two hours later when an alarm clock went off within him. He sat upright. Now was the time. The white man must be sleeping. He squinted carefully across the compartment, studying his friend's face.

As the train rattled around a corner, a shaft of moonlight played across the sahib's eyes. The white man was awake! Bimal could feel the sahib looking deep into his soul. The two men exchanged quick glances, but neither broke the silence.

Bimal leaned back to the wall. He would wait. *There are twelve hours in the long ride to Purulia. The white man will eventually sleep.*

He was not afraid of death. Bimal's mother had died when he was very young. It had been almost a blessing when his father had died. He really was not sad. His father had never cared about the family. At sixteen Bimal was alone in Calcutta. He had been frightened at first, but eventually he had conquered his fears.

Calcutta was a great city to Bimal. He was in love with it. He thought of it as a great body. The people were the blood stream; they moved from one end of the city to the other in constant motion. The streets were the veins and arteries. The blood stream carried life to every corner of the body. Bimal knew that Calcutta would not miss him; he was only a tiny part of that great body. Every day blood cells were dying and new ones were born. But it had always given him satisfaction to know that he was part of something much bigger than himself. *Calcutta will last forever,* he had often mused.

The night wore on, but the sahib did not sleep. Though Bimal was tortured with thoughts of the future, he thought about the past too. He thought about the war. He remembered terrible battles when the shelling had been at its worst. He hadn't tasted fear as he did now, though. It was a fear much worse than the fear of death: the fear that he would live—in constant hell.

"You should sleep," the white man whispered. He spoke very gently, but his words shattered the silence.

"Yes, I will sleep."

Bimal smiled to himself. *What a strange creature the pastor is,* he thought. Never had he known a friend like him. No one could have such a friend as his.

Bimal had told the story of the white man to so many people for so many years it was like staring at a photograph of a friend. Pretty soon you could no longer see the person, only the photograph. Now he thought carefully, to make it all alive again.

The white man had wandered through Bimal's bustee one afternoon in 1959, a crowd of curious children trailing him through the alleyways. He had found a poor family of seven people living in a room so small they had to take turns sleeping. The father lay on a cot in an alleyway. He was blind, helpless to care for his dirty and hungry family, and now he had been overcome by a terrible fever. Everyone expected him to die. His wife was praying that he would be reborn a rich man.

The sahib had announced that he would help the family, and the crowd had cheered. The old man was taken away.

Only days later, he returned. As he reentered his neighborhood, a great crowd began to gather. They marched with him through the alleys.

"You are well?"

"Yes, I am well, thank you."

"You look very good."

"They gave me good medicine!"

"Can you see?" "He isn't blind!" "What did they do for you?"

A great tide of excitement swept through the bustee. Dozens of different stories had been told. The word reached Bimal: "Your uncle, they have fixed his eyes! Your old uncle, he can see now!"

Bimal had rushed through the streets and the crowded alleyways to the old man's home. There his uncle stood, straight and tall like a learned guru teaching his followers. Bimal was astonished.

"The God of Jesus has given me new eyes! It is the God of Jesus!" the old man shouted. Bimal had cringed with embarrassment, but the crowd had seemed willing to listen.

Privately, he made the old man tell him the story over and over.

"They told me that Jesus can do anything. They said that if I believed, Jesus would let me see again. They washed me and I could see shadows and light."

"They operated on you. They operated, right?"

"No! They washed me. Each morning they washed my eyes, and I kept seeing clearer. I can see you now."

Bimal had determined to talk to the white man. He had found the church and the pastor. But there were to be no miracles for Bimal, only work. Bimal smiled to himself when he thought about his friend.

This pastor had lived in India a long time, but still had not learned to respect all its traditions. His people worked in a ditch, building his new church. People of all castes worked together, and the women served them sandwiches and drink.

Bimal had shuddered. It was outrageous, this important man pounding the foundation with businessmen from his congregation all helping. Yet drawn to this white man, Bimal soon found himself in the large hole pounding the mud around the bricks. The man was often at his side, thanking him and commending him for his humility.

The large complex on Royd Street grew. There were food programs for the children, a home for drug addicts, a school with sixteen hundred students, a busy but small hospital, and a large Christian church. Soon after a building was completed, it was jammed with activity.

Bimal, a Navy veteran with great organizational talents, was soon absorbed by the growing Royd Street mission. More and more the sahib consulted him, until Bimal found himself an intimate advisor and a foreman for many of his projects.

Sometimes they talked late into the night. The white man often spoke of his dream of a great hospital and a new chapel. "I want to live to see this whole neighborhood taken care of spiritually and physically."

For seven years Bimal watched the parade of humanity which lined up in front of the pastor's office door. He heard the sermons preached each night before large crowds. He saw the white man pick up the helpless and give them new lives. He observed the sahib's uncanny ability to spot the lazy and corrupt. He watched while he cried with the children, and Bimal felt himself drawn to worship the white man's God.

It was at this peaceful time in Bimal's life that an evil messenger came to announce that Bimal's life was over, that he had begun to die. He had seen this messenger before, had seen him stalk the bustees picking out his victims at random.

The Hindus believe only an evil person can receive this evil messenger, so will throw their own children, wife or husband into the streets to rot. Even the untouchables won't drag the bodies away, and thieves leave their clothes alone.

Bimal had seen this messenger do his work. Once he had struck a very close friend, a commando in the Navy, a very strong man. First his eyes began to discharge yellow pus, then the carnivorous messenger took control, feasting on this strong man and leaving behind a helpless vegetable without eyes, or nose, or hands. Bimal had despised his own friend when this had happened, and after one visit, had refused to see him again.

There were many tormenting nights before Bimal slipped out of the Royd Street compound to visit another hospital far across Calcutta. He waited for hours; when they called his name, he almost bolted.

"It is your liver," the old doctor said. He knew what Bimal had been fearing, so he patted his shoulder and chuckled. "Only your liver. It is not operating as it should. That's why you have these spots all over your arms."

Bimal relaxed.

"I'll give you some pills. This will clear up in a few weeks."

Only days later the messenger was back, laughing his shrill laugh and promising Bimal a horrible, living death that would take away his friends and leave him alone to rot in a gutter. The blemishes were still there, and they stayed for weeks.

Finally there was pain. There had never been pain before. Flashbacks of his old Navy companion began to haunt him. Vividly he remembered the screams and anguish. Bimal had not cared about his friend; he had watched him suffer with contempt. "He is surely being punished for sins of a previous lifetime," that young Hindu reasoned. An older Bimal agreed.

Terrible scenes filled his mind. He could not sleep; he could only see his friend covered with open sores and screaming out to him. During the day as he worked, Bimal could feel the conversations of others around him. He knew that they could see the changing colors of his skin and imagined they would soon throw him out.

One afternoon they called to him. "The pastor wants you. The pastor wants you!"

Bimal was startled. His mind raced ahead. *Where will I go? What can I do? There is nothing to fear. They are wrong. It is only a problem with my liver—the doctor has said so.*

"Come in," the pastor greeted, as though he were a special guest.

"Sit here in this chair by the window, Bimal."

Bimal nodded.

"You are a very sick man, Bimal," the white man had spoken with great gentleness. "I want you to come with me to our doctor. I want him to examine you."

The room became silent, as if they awaited the verdict of a jury. Both the white man and Bimal had known what the doctor's judgment would be. The loneliness that engulfed him in that silent room had never left.

There was a long howl from the train whistle. Bimal sat upright. He had almost drifted to sleep with his thoughts. He studied the sahib sitting opposite him. It was very dark. The train was racing through the countryside. Occasionally there was a glow from a gas lantern in the distance, but the lights were barely visible from the fast-moving train.

The moon had begun its descent, which meant that Bimal was now visible to the white man. Bimal strained his eyes, but he could see only the darkened outline of his friend. He moved away from the window.

Now he could hear the sahib breathing deeply. *He is asleep.* Bimal stood quietly and leaned closer to his friend. He was wrong; the white man was still awake. He was staring back at him curiously. Bimal sat back quickly, disappointed and embarrassed.

*What am I going to do? This cannot go on. In a few hours it will be daylight. The sahib must sleep soon.* Bimal stared back out into the night. Once again his thoughts returned to Calcutta, and for the hundreth time he recounted the events of that horrible day when the pastor had driven him through the crowded streets to the doctor.

There had been no conversation. Muffled Calcutta street noises had filtered into the automobile, giving Bimal a dream-like sensation that he was far away. In the examination room, the doctor took only a few moments. He exchanged glances with the white man. Bimal tried to read their faces, but both men avoided his eyes.

"May I speak with you alone?"

Bimal looked up. The doctor was speaking to the sahib. The pastor looked at his Indian friend and nodded toward the door. Bimal stepped into an outer office.

The white man emerged within seconds. His face was ashen. There were tears in his eyes. He walked quickly past Bimal and out into the street.

"What did he say?" Bimal hurried after him, his heart beating rapidly with fear.

The white man ignored his question. "Get in the car. Let's go."

"Where are we going?"

"We are going to another doctor!"

"Why?"

"I want a dermatologist to see you."

Bimal broke into tears. The pastor did not have to say any more. *Oh, God, do not let it be,* Bimal prayed. *Do not let it be.*

The doctor's office was filled with people. The pastor spoke to a nurse. Come on, the pastor waved Bimal in. He arranged for the doctor to see him immediately.

When it was over, Bimal waited in the car. It was hot, and he began to sweat. He watched some children playing nearby, but nothing could keep his attention long. Eventually the white man emerged from the office. *Oh, God, if it is not so, I will praise you forever. I will tell everyone of the miracle you have done for me. I will become a Christian! Yes, I will become a Christian!*

The pastor slipped into the seat. Before he spoke, Bimal could feel the words. A terrible depression sprang from somewhere inside. Neither man looked at the other. In the midst of seven million people, they were in a world of their own.

"Bimal, my friend, you have a very bad case of leprosy."

The Indian sat still for a moment. Then his body began to shake. He tried to maintain control. His lips trembled; his legs and arms shook.

The white man turned away. "Oh, Jesus," he whispered.

"Pastor, is it very bad," he whispered.

"Bimal, it is very bad. Very, very serious. It is highly contagious. The doctor says you must go to a leprosarium. That is your only chance."

"Pastor, in that case, I am a dead man. Tell my family that I have disappeared. I want to go now. I want to go alone."

The white man grabbed him. "No, I will not let you go. We will face this thing together. You are my friend; I will not let you do anything foolish."

46

Bimal began to shake again.

"I will not let you leave this car!" the white man shouted at him. "You are going to face this, and you are going to live. Straighten up!"

Bimal broke into sobs. Tears flooded his face, and his whole body convulsed. The missionary clutched him tightly and sobbed with him.

"We are friends, Bimal. We are friends. We will face this together."

The missionary had made all the arrangements. He had taken Bimal into his own home. He had been careful never to leave Bimal alone. Throughout the long, monotonous trip to Purulia, he had not taken his eyes off his friend.

The night eventually passed. As the two men sat staring out the train windows, a band of light appeared on the horizon and rose like a curtain in the east. Bimal knew his suicide plans must be postponed. The pastor's eyes had been locked in on him like radar. He was determined to see his friend safely to Purulia. *Eventually the pastor will have to leave,* Bimal thought to himself. *I also am determined. I will not spend the rest of my life in a leprosarium.*

# 5

"Let's go," the white man was standing next to Bimal. The train had stopped. Bimal avoided the white man's eyes, for he was now sure his friend could read his thoughts.

"Where will we go first?" Bimal grabbed his luggage.

"I have friends here. We will meet them."

Bimal was tormented by the beauty of the morning. The birds were singing; the sky was blue and clear. As they arrived at a large house, Bimal hesitated on the steps. "I will wait for you here."

"Go on." The missionary ignored his protest and shoved him lightly.

"Come in. Come in. We have been expecting you." A large white woman greeted them.

"We wanted the exercise, so we walked."

"Mark, it's so good to see you. How's Huldah?"

The white man smiled and slumped into a big stuffed chair, "Oh, she's fine."

"And this is Bimal," the large woman took his hand. Bimal was overwhelmed with confusion. Was this calm atmosphere for his benefit? *I am a leper. I don't belong in this house.*

"I've heard all about you," the woman said. She patted Bimal's shoulder. "We are praying for you."

Bimal was overcome by his reception. He bowed awkwardly.

"Before you go, you must have breakfast. It is all ready. The others are waiting."

They sat at the table. Bimal was very tense. *I cannot believe this. I am a leper. I do not belong here. I cannot eat at this table. Westerners are strange.*

The missionaries talked, but Bimal could not hear them. His thoughts were far away.

After breakfast they walked to the leprosarium. To the missionary, it was a long walk. He was sweating profusely, wishing he had accepted his friend's offer to drive them. To Bimal the walk was fast. He did not see any of the people around him. He saw only one thing. As the two men came out of a narrow, dark street, they had turned a corner into sunlight. There glittering in the sun, only a hundred yards away, was the gate of the leper colony. Bimal had never seen it before, but he knew what it was.

*It is my grave,* he shuddered. *The Hindus are right, you cannot change fate.*

Bimal had never imagined what it would be like to enter the gates of the leprosarium. He had promised himself he would die first. It felt as though he were not even there, as though this Indian who walked to his death were a stranger—someone he had never known, and someone he could not understand. It was as though he were being dropped into the ocean from one of the great ships he had worked on during the war, with huge weights chained to his legs, dropping deeper and deeper. The white man prayed with him and they walked together as Bimal was moved from one room to the next. There were tests and examinations. There were papers to fill out. Bimal struggled to remain coherent for his friend's sake. He felt tired and harassed. The day seemed to drag on forever.

Then it was over. It was night, and he had been sleeping. He was in a very long, narrow cottage. He wondered when the white man had left and what his last words to him had been. Bimal fell back on his cot. At least he was alone. He wanted to be alone. He felt peace.

In the morning his peace was shattered. Only inches from his face a man's foot dangled. There was only one large toe on the foot. It was split in two by a cavern of pus. Bimal bolted upright. The flies stirred from his sudden movement, and then settled back to the foot, the eyelids, the mouth of the man lying next to him.

Bimal wondered if his neighbor were dead, but not wishing to demonstrate ignorance, he said nothing. The whole room was watching him.

The man across from him nodded. Bimal stared with horror at the face which had no nose. Instead, there was a grotesquely shaped, infected hole in its place. Bimal looked away, making a mental note not to stare at their deformities, but to look only at their eyes.

Bimal was free to roam anywhere in the large compound as long as he didn't leave the colony. He moved away from the little groups of visiting inmates and walked the length of the yard. Near the fence there was a huge rock where Bimal sat quietly. From his vantage point, he surveyed the buildings. He looked at the other lepers; from this distance he could not see their deformities. They looked like people.

He glanced across the fence, grasping for a new method of suicide. The night of rest had weakened his resolve to kill himself. Now he found he really wanted to live, wanted to be free. He sat on the rock for more than an hour and wept.

Sometime during that hour, the white man joined him and they sat, arm in arm, weeping together.

"Bimal, now is the time to accept Jesus." The white man said. "Jesus is the Son of God. He can help you."

Bimal remembered his old uncle. He wondered if it were all true that in some form or another Jesus really lived. The Christians taught that He had a new body. That was not difficult for a Hindu to accept. But did Jesus have power? Was he really God?

"Bimal." The white man spoke as if he were about to reveal a secret. He stared at one of the fence posts until Bimal thought it would disintegrate under the power of the sahib's eyes.

"One very special time Jesus helped me," the pastor said softly. "No one else could have. It was very black and very dark where I was. I cannot explain it all to you." His voice sounded far away, as he re-lived the past.

"There was great fear. I was afraid of myself. It was getting very dark inside. I cried out to God, but it seemed as though He couldn't hear me. But finally, God heard me, and Jesus saved me. Bimal, Jesus will never fail you. You must trust Him. The whole world will fail you, but Jesus will never fail."

"Help me, Jesus." Bimal spoke it very softly, so the white man could not hear him. But each time he repeated it, his voice became stronger. "Help me, Jesus. Help me, Jesus." Bimal shouted aloud, "Jesus, you are the Son of God. You are the Son of God. Help me!"

The white man stood, looked at the leprosarium, and said, "Satan, you will not keep him here. Someday he will walk out of this place."

Bimal was suddenly overwhelmed. His insides seemed to convulse in emotion. To this day he weeps when he describes the sensation.

"Suddenly, God was there within me. I felt great joy, but mostly great power. The color of my skin had not changed, yet I felt peace. Leprosy meant nothing to me. In that moment, I felt stronger than leprosy. I felt stronger than the pastor, the fence, the buildings, the other inmates. I was stronger than them all. When days came that I weakened and became discouraged, I would pray again and that strength always came back to me."

They walked arm in arm, triumphantly across the yard. The white man was beaming now, the Indian's face was aglow. Standing beside Bimal's bed they said farewell.

"I will be out of here soon. I will be back in Calcutta some day."

The pastor smiled, then he grabbed Bimal's hands. "Thank you, Jesus," he said, shutting his eyes very tightly in a prayer. "Thank you, Jesus, you never fail."

The leprosarium soon learned that one of its new arrivals claimed to have experienced great spiritual power. Bimal was quick to explain what little he knew of Christianity, and what had seemed to happen to him when he prayed.

"You are very weak," the doctor had told him. "Your body may be much too frail to handle such strong medicine."

"I am in the hands of the greatest of all powers," Bimal replied.

The doctor had heard comments about this Bengali patient. "And what power is this?"

"Jesus Christ."

"Do you think He can cure your leprosy?"

"Doctor, Jesus Christ has already cured my soul, and He has cured my mind. I do not fear leprosy any longer."

"Well, that's good," the doctor said, "because you have a very severe case, and you will probably spend the rest of your life here."

Bimal did not flinch, but smiled. "I do not want to insult you, but if your medicine fails, Jesus will not fail. He has cured my soul and mind as signs that He will also cure my body. I shall walk out of this place, and you will see it happen."

The doctor shook his head. "Bimal, I like you," he said. "You are a remarkable man."

By the end of the year, Bimal's dosage of Dapsone Sulphate was increased from five milligrams to 300 milligrams per week. There were no bad effects. The doctor was pleased.

Each week Bimal received a letter from the white man's wife. He would read the letters over and over again. He would meditate for days upon her words of advice. Soon the others around him demanded to know more of Bimal's faith.

They gathered around him when a letter arrived and he would read it aloud, explaining to them what it meant.

Bimal's attitude became a powerful tonic for the entire cottage. They asked him to speak before they slept at night. When pain was unbearable or when someone died he would find an old letter from the missionary's wife and read it aloud to everyone again.

One day a special letter came. It was the second one to arrive that week.

Dear Bimal,

We have been praying. Some of us feel that God is healing your body.

We want you to know that we are banking your pay check for you each month in your absence. The money will be waiting for you when you return home to us.

Also, we are holding your job until you return home. Please have faith that God will heal you.

Sincerely,
Huldah

They were all astonished by the letter. A leper is an outcast to most Hindus. They could not imagine such devoted friends. Bimal read the letter again and again. His friends stared at him. Rashid was shaking his head. He was always amazed when Bimal read his letters.

"White men are not that generous!" someone shouted.

"You are right," Bimal shouted back. "White men are evil, and we are evil. It is Jesus who is good. It is Jesus inside my pastor who is generous, and I have Jesus in me."

"I want Jesus," Rashid said. There was silence.

Bimal looked at Rashid. He was very ugly. His face was distorted, and he had stumps instead of hands and feet. Rashid lay all day and night upon his cot, yet he was very strong in other ways. He never complained. He never cried out in pain.

"Yes, I will give you Jesus," Bimal said. He prayed, and Rashid became the first of many converts.

After the special letter, Bimal thought often about going home. He prayed for a miracle. But one day Rashid died. They had a great celebration. "Rashid is in a wonderful paradise. He has a new body. He is not a leper any longer!" Bimal changed his prayer after that. *I do not care how long I stay here, just help me to teach the others about Jesus.*

Winter nights were cold, yet they were fondly remembered by everyone the following summer. With summer heat came flies; they swarmed through the cottages, feasting on the delicacy of decaying flesh. Temperatures reached 125 degrees. When it was almost unbearable, fall came again, and the temperatures dropped.

There was no break in routine, day after day, month after month. Changes only took place in the lepers themselves. Hands and feet withered away. Ears and noses disappeared. Sores moved like glaciers from one part of the body to the next. You could not see them move, but you would remember that a year ago they had been in different places.

It happened to everyone but Bimal. Every three months the doctor would examine him. The report was always the same. "You are doing very well," the doctor would laugh. "I don't know if it is my medicine or yours."

One day in May, Bimal was summoned to the doctor's office. The doctor stared at some papers in his hands. "Bimal, how long have you been here?"

"Two years, sir."

"That's what this says." The doctor tapped his papers, then he turned to Bimal abruptly. "How would you like to go home?"

Bimal was stunned. He had noticed that his condition had improved, but had never allowed himself the luxury of such thoughts.

"Did you hear me?" The doctor smiled, obviously delighted that he had surprised the usually cocky Bengali.

"When?"

"We will know soon. Let me check you today, then come in again tomorrow, and I will let you know how long it will be."

After the examination, Bimal rushed back to his cottage. Kanu stopped him. "What is it? What has happened?"

"I am going home!" As Bimal spoke, he realized it was true: he would be in Calcutta soon. The darkest trial of his live was over. He wept with joy.

Kanu's eyes sparkled. "It is your God. Your God has done this for you. When do you leave?"

"I don't know, maybe a few months. But I'm going home!"

Kanu led Bimal through the cottages past row after row of beds. The news spread before them. Bimal was a celebrity. They reached out and touched him; it was as close as many of them would ever come to freedom. There were congratulations. There were more tears.

"Kanu," Bimal confided privately. "I don't know if my tomorrow will ever come."

"It will come. It will come. You need to listen to some of your own advice. Tomorrow will come."

Bimal awakened early. He waited outside the examination room several hours before the doctor arrived.

"Bimal, you are the first case we have had like this. The minimum stay here is five to six years. When you arrived, I did not expect you ever to get out alive. You have been here not quite two years. You are a remarkable man."

"Doctor, I am an evil man, but God is very powerful."

"Yes, I know." The doctor smiled. "We are releasing you today."

The Indian broke into tears. It had always been important for him to maintain control in front of the doctor, but he could not restrain himself.

A crowd gathered around his bed as he packed. He passed out all of his religious tracts and some of his letters. They grabbed for them as though they were sacred relics. "Remember all I have told you. Jesus will never fail you."

Everyone in the cottage cheered loudly.

"Leprosy is nothing to Jesus. He is more powerful than leprosy."

They cheered again. They stood on their beds and cheered. Twisted old men, who would never leave the colony alive, cheered. They stuck their stubs in the air and waved them defiantly.

Bimal wept again. "I will write you."

"And we will read your letters aloud," Kanu said.

Bimal picked up his luggage and ran triumphantly across the compound. "The God of Jesus has set me free!" he shouted loudly. He turned and looked at the hundreds of faces peering at him from windows. He was not embarrassed; he was proud. "It is the God of Jesus! He is the one." He shouted at them. "The God of Jesus has set me free!"

The lepers watched him pass through the gate. They watched him until he disappeared into the crowded streets of Purulia.

The pastor was seated at his desk. He looked up. His mouth dropped open in astonishment. He jumped to his feet.

"Bimal!"

The Indian stood in the doorway, laughing, all he owned dangled in bundles from both hands.

"Bimal!"

"My pastor, I am home. I am home to stay."

"Bimal!" The white man grabbed him. They embraced each other, laughing. The pastor leaned out the door and shouted across the compound. "Hey!" People could hear his voice a block away. "Hey!" he shouted urgently. "Hey!"

A young man came dashing out of the print shop. Maybe the pastor had caught his hand in a fan.

A secretary came running down the stairs. Breathlessly she burst into the room and saw Bimal. "Oh!" she gasped. "Oh!" She ran out of the office shouting, "He's back, he's back. Bimal is home!"

The missionary's wife stepped to the door of her office. "Who's back?" she asked.

"Bimal. Bimal is back."

The white woman raced across the compound to the pastor's office.

Bimal was seated calmly in the middle of a crowd of teachers and children. Some of them were close friends. The secretary was crying. The pastor smiled hugely.

"Jesus will never fail you." Bimal told the crowd. "He will never fail you."

"Praise God," the pastor said. "Praise God." He looked at his wife standing in the doorway. "Oh, Huldah, this is a wonderful day. This is a wonderful day! Jesus never fails!"

*Rajendra*

# 6

Rajendra was a frightening sight. The most imaginative make-up artist could not have created him. He was filthy. His skin was covered with running sores. His teeth were stained and rotting. The rags he wore seemed to have sweat glands giving off a sensuous odor of filth.

Lately, Rajendra had taken to treating his hair with a rich-looking cream he had found in a junk heap near his block. He did not know exactly what it was, but thought perhaps the treatment would help stop his balding and its strong odor might drive out some of the insect life.

Rajendra's greatest frustration was loneliness. At times he had reached out to others, groping for some kind of companionship, but there had been none. Rajendra was twenty-seven years old. That was the problem: he was too old to be pitied. Just the same, he needed help. He was dying.

When he was younger, there had always been people to take care of him. His mother already had six children, and they were starving. Rajendra miraculously lived through that first year. He was already demonstrating an uncanny ability to survive the most adverse conditions. Then his mother persuaded a friend to take him for awhile. By the time Rajendra was seven years old, he had lived all over the streets of Calcutta. He would stay in a neighborhood long enough to develop an adult friend—someone to talk to him and give him scraps of food at least once a day. These sponsors invariably lost interest. When little Rajendra began to suffer hunger pains, he would wander on until someone new discovered him.

Occasionally some well intentioned individual would return him to his mother—no easy task, for in the spreading bustees of Calcutta, it is difficult to find someone like her. Rajendra had never known his father. On one of his short stays at home he asked about him. "Your father died before you were born," he was told. He never knew if it were true.

Eventually his mother discovered the perfect solution. She gave her son to some Roman Catholic sisters. It was quite a break for the little street urchin.

The amazed sisters soon realized the child was highly talented mathematically. He advanced quickly with very little instruction. Within a few years, he was devouring old algebra and geometry textbooks. His grades in other subjects, though poor at first, began to improve too. His desire to understand the mathematics textbooks prompted him to take his English classes more seriously.

During these years, Rajendra began to learn how unique he was. When school was dismissed for holidays, the other children cheered, but Rajendra had no reason to celebrate; he had no home. Even the orphans at the school had older brothers or sisters, or aunts and uncles they would visit. Rajendra hardly knew his mother. He could not even remember the names of his brothers and sisters. As far as he knew there was no uncle or aunt. He had no one who wanted him. He sometimes told the sisters he was leaving to visit his mother. Actually, Rajendra's mother had left Calcutta shortly after she had given him away. When Rajendra learned this on one of his excursions from St. Mary's, he ran from the bustee in tears. He slept near a railroad track that night.

Thereafter on holidays, Rajendra would wander aimlessly through the streets of Calcutta. He was too proud to tell the sisters he had nowhere to go. Sometimes Rajendra returned to school near starvation. When one of the sisters became inquisitive he told her that his family was poor.

Rajendra began to resent the other children. He began to despise the sisters. They were continually talking about things he did not understand. He was clever enough to realize that he needed the sisters, but he didn't see any need for the other children. His hostility surfaced.

On many occasions Rajendra was severely beaten by other boys. Usually they were fights which he himself provoked. Rajendra always fought alone; there were never any allies. Once during a holiday he was set upon by a gang of men. When he fought them, they beat him and left him for dead.

Thereafter, Rajendra feared leaving the school when vacations came. He finally told the sisters that his mother had moved away, so they agreed to let him stay.

Rajendra's personality began to change. He discovered that he had the ability to practically disappear. If he wanted to, he could simply withdraw within himself, and no one would bother him.

His closest friend during this period was an old algebra textbook. Rajendra had cut his intellectual teeth on the book. He had learned English by reading and rereading the text. The book brought some continuity to his life. The first pages of numbers and formulas spoke to him of his early years at St. Mary's. Rajendra kept the book near his pallet at night. Sometimes he would casually flip through the pages in the moonlight, spotting an old formula and feeling comforted, as if he were visiting an old friend.

When Rajendra left St. Mary's at twelve, he had one request. He wanted to keep the old textbook. He asked one of the sisters who had treated him kindly. "No, we must use this to teach other children," she said, taking the book from him. Rajendra was angry and jealous at the thought that someone else would have his textbook.

Life at St. Mary's did not prepare an orphan for life on the streets of Calcutta. Now that he was older, there would be no sponsors. He first worked with a crew digging the foundation for a building. Rajendra considered himself lucky, because though he was given no money, once a day he was fed a bowl of rice with the workmen. Within a few days he was told to leave. "You're not worth the rice we give you!"

For several weeks Rajendra wandered through the streets begging for food. When his next job opportunity came, he was determined to put all his effort into it. The work was strenuous, and Rajendra's body was not able to hold up. It had been pampered at St. Mary's by two meals a day. One bowl of rice did not give him sufficient energy to meet the demands of hard labor. Just when he was ready to quit, his employer announced that the work was over. The project was abandoned. It was back to the streets for Rajendra.

Eventually, he developed a reputation as a hard worker. He began to earn some rupees of his own. At first there were only enough to buy extra food. Then he accumulated a surplus. More than anything else, Rajendra wanted shoes. He had grown so tall his rags no longer properly covered him, so he also needed clothes.

A man in his neighborhood agreed to sell him a pair of his son's shoes and some old clothing. Rajendra paid in cash. Later the man claimed that the items had been stolen. No one would believe Rajendra's story. He had a hard and suspicious personality; no one really knew him. He considered fleeing to another street, but he reasoned that the police would find him, so he decided to return the shoes and clothing.

The neighbor was shamed by this action. He constantly apologized to Rajendra whenever he would see him. "I wouldn't have done it, but my children are starving. I am sorry."

Rajendra would always reply politely, "I understand."

The old neighbor never returned the money, and eventually he began to resent the young man's presence on the street. Rajendra seemed to carry himself with dignity in spite of the fact that he slept with two dogs in a gutter. The old man encouraged the neighbors to believe that Rajendra was a thief. In spite of the fact that he wore everything he owned on his back, the neighbors accepted this verdict. Rajendra was driven from the neighborhood.

When the Indian army began action in World War II, Rajendra enlisted. The army opened the world to him. He experienced luxuries that he had never known before. To him the food rations were extravagant. In Cairo he was stationed in a barracks on a cot. He slept with warm blankets.

Mostly World War II exposed him to people. In his uniform, Rajendra was treated as an equal. He was included in conversations. He would rarely say anything for fear of displaying ignorance on some subject, but he did listen. He listened and he learned.

Before the war had ended, some of his army companions discovered what a brilliant mathematician he was. They only stumbled onto the fact accidentally, and Rajendra himself was surprised to find that his skill was so great. Occasionally a soldier posed a mathematical problem, and Rajendra would quickly spit back the answer like a computer. Everyone would laugh. Sometimes a skeptic would work the problem out himself. Rajendra was always correct.

In 1945 the war ended. Rajendra's pleasurable army life was over. He was overcome with loneliness. For days he wandered the streets of Bombay, seeking work. Unlike the other soldiers, he had saved some of his money. He had not squandered it on prostitutes and liquor, so Rajendra had something to live on. But it would not last long. Suddenly, he had an idea. He would find his mother and brothers and sisters.

It would not be easy, and it might cost him all of his money, but it would be worth it. They would help him find work. Rajendra bought a train ticket to Calcutta to see if he could pick up the trail.

His search lasted three months and took him to Madras. He imagined that his family would be surprised and pleased to see him. He envisioned a family meal together as he gave a detailed account of his adventures in the army. However, in Madras he lost the trail. They had moved from their one room apartment. The manager insisted on a fee before he would reveal their forwarding address.

"But I have no money. It is all gone."

"If you want to see your mother badly enough, you will get a job and pay me."

"I can't get a job here. There is not even enough work for me in Calcutta where people know me. Can you help me get a job?"

"I manage these apartments. I cannot run all over the city trying to find you a job. Anyway, how do I know that you are telling me the truth?"

Rajendra camped across the street from the apartments. Within days he was starving to death. Attempts to find work failed. He considered stealing food, but he had never stolen anything in his life, and he resisted the impulse.

Eventually the manager gave in. He had been watching Rajendra from his room across the street. When he realized how desperate the young man was, he came to him one morning with an address written on a piece of paper. "Here, you damn dog!" The manager peeled off ten rupees and threw them at him. Evidently Rajendra had bothered his conscience.

With his mother's address clutched to his bosom, Rajendra found new strength. He ran through the streets of Madras searching frantically for the right address. It was six in the evening when he found it. He stumbled up a flight of stairs and knocked on a door.

Rajendra's mother lived in a two-room home. By western standards, it was inadequate: there was no toilet and no running water. To Rajendra it was luxurious. He was surprised and relieved to see his mother living so comfortably. She was dressed in a yellow sari. Rajendra did not recognize her, but he knew she was his mother.

She looked at him with disapproval and motioned for him to sit down. Another young man entered the room. Rajendra presumed that it was one of his brothers. There was silence.

"I've been in the army. I was stationed in Cairo."

There was no response. His mother and the young man only stared at him.

"I did quite well in the Army."

Rajendra felt self-conscious in his rags. "I spent everything coming to see you, I will be getting a job right away."

There was no answer, only silence.

"How do I know you are my son?" she said sternly.

Rajendra looked into his mother's face, then to the young man. He did not know how to answer. He realized now that his appearance had disgraced them.

"I am very good in mathematics. I have considered going into accounting."

"You're filthy," the young man said.

Rajendra looked deep into his mother's eyes. "You know I am your son."

She turned away. "You are a disgrace to me. You are a disgrace to your brothers and sisters. You live on the street. Do you think that is something you can hide?"

Now Rajendra was silent.

His mother looked at him long and hard. "If you use our name, it will ruin us. Is that what you have come to do? Go ahead. To me you are not Rajendra. I don't know who you are, and I don't care." She pointed her finger at him, "You are not my son. Now get out."

Rajendra stood and stumbled backwards. He was stunned. A tall man walked in from the other room, perhaps another brother.

"Out!" the man shouted.

"I haven't eaten in several days."

His mother hissed, "That's why you came here."

"Out!" the man shouted.

Rajendra took one long look at his mother. He knew that he would soon forget what she looked like, but he wanted to remember as long as possible.

"Out!" the man shouted.

Rajendra stumbled down the stairs. He never saw his family again.

During the next years, Rajendra almost died. He returned to Calcutta where he worked for fifteen- to twenty-day contracts at various hard-labor jobs. In between jobs, he would live off his meager savings, sometimes going without food for days at a time.

It was in the midst of one of these bouts with disaster that Rajendra was overcome by knowledge that he was going to die. He had been out of money for days. The effects of his life had been creeping up on him for months. His body was covered with sores. His hair was falling out in little clumps. The cream he was using to treat his scalp only added to his hideous appearance. He begged for food, but only received enough to keep him hungry.

Lately, he had begun to pick over the garbage. Sometimes after eating the wrong things he would vomit it all up. He would continue to retch an hour later until his sides ached with pain.

Rajendra had continued to pursue work. "There's a man on Victoria Street who needs workers," he would be told. It was always a lie to get rid of him. Usually the street address did not exist, but Rajendra couldn't afford to take that chance. He would wander from one end of Calcutta to the other. He would wait for hours to meet someone who had no intention of keeping an appointment. Finally, convinced he would soon die, Rajendra looked about for a suitable place to sleep forever.

# 7

One morning a sahib in a western suit walked briskly down Park Street, in the heart of Calcutta. He seemed preoccupied, completely unresponsive to sights and sounds around him. Then he stopped. He looked at a group of people camped on the sidewalk next to a tall building. A daughter was deeply engrossed in picking the lice out of her mother's hair. Nearby a man was selling cigarettes. Another man slumped against the wall, his body covered with sores. The only sign of life was the grease dripping from his hair onto his rags. It was the sight of this beggar that had stopped the white man in his tracks.

He stared intently at the young man in rags, like a jeweler examining a precious stone by turning it over and over in his fingers. The beggar was unconscious.

"Oh, God," the sahib gasped. He stooped next to the beggar and pulled apart his rags to reveal a chest full of sores. "Oh, Jesus, I know that you love him, Jesus. I know that you died for this man, Jesus. What can we do?"

The white man stared at the hideous sight. *There is no room at the compound,* he thought. *We are already full. He is in no shape to work, but I just can't let him die.* He looked at his watch. *It's almost nine o'clock. I've got to keep my appointment.*

The white man turned to the woman nearby. "Do you know this man?"

She only grunted.

*Maybe she knows Hindi.* "Do you know this man?" the sahib said in Hindi.

"No," the woman snapped back in English. "No."

The white man stared vacantly across the street. Wheels were turning in his mind. For a long time he stared, thinking. Finally he spoke aloud, "I am come that you might have life, and have it more abundantly." They were the words of Jesus. He said them again, this time much louder. "I am come that you might have life, an abundant life."

The white man put his arms around the unconscious beggar, "Jesus has come to give you an abundant life, an abundant life." It was like a child speaking to a doll, for the beggar was nearly lifeless and could not hear him. The white man closed his eyes, "Now God, keep him here. Don't let him wander off some place. If you want me to help him, keep him right here. Just put your arms around him, Jesus. Don't let him die. You have taken care of him all these years. Now keep him alive for just a while longer."

An hour later the white man returned. He was accompanied by an Indian. "Bimal, help me get these rags off him."

"He may have a terrible disease."

The missionary turned to the Indian. "You once had a terrible disease," he scowled.

Bimal reluctantly began to pull the dirty rags off the beggar.

"Now this will hurt you," the missionary said. He began to bathe the beggar in a clear-looking solution. The beggar did not cry out; he did not flinch—he did not regain consciousness.

Bimal disappeared down the street, then returned with a cup of hot tea.

Rajendra awakened to the wonderful aroma of this tea. The cup was right at his lips. He began to sip slowly. He was groggy, still uncomprehending. A white man with enormous glasses was staring right into his face and mumbling words from the Bible. "Woe to you who are well-fed now, for you shall be hungry." The man's voice was filled with emotion, and the cup he was holding to Rajendra's lips was trembling.

The sahib stood and placed his hands on the beggar's head. His western suit was now stained with water and solutions. The white man prayed, "Jesus, may your peace come to this man. Send your Holy Spirit to him now. Never leave him." The white man interrupted his prayer, he could not finish. He looked down at Rajendra and started shaking his head. "Let's go Bimal," and they disappeared down the street.

With a belly full of tea, Rajendra fell into a deep sleep. Later he called it "the most wonderful sleep of my life." He awakened to discover that his visitors had left behind more tea and a little box full of cakes and fruit. It was more than Rajendra's shrunken stomach could possibly hold, so he gave some to one of the pye-dogs who had occasionally shared food with him. He was dressed in clean clothes. They were much too big, especially in the waist, but there was a string which he could use as a belt. His rags were gone, probably burned. The jar of cream was still there. Rajendra felt his hair. It had been crudely cut and shampooed.

He felt so clean and so full that once again he drifted to sleep. The warm sun covered him like a blanket. He did not awaken until the next morning.

"Do you want a job?" An Indian man was shaking him. "Do you want a job? We need lots of help. We are working over on Royd Street."

"Yes," Rajendra sat upright. He was amazed to feel so strong.

The walls were going up on a new building at the mission compound. Rajendra didn't see the white man for several days, but he suspected he was responsible for arranging his new work.

As the weeks passed, Rajendra grew stronger. He began to despise the whole set up. He resented the generous portions of food he was served. He was offended by the easy work assigned him.

The white man must have sensed this. One day he called Rajendra into his office. "Either you are going to have to do your share of the work or get out." Rajendra stared back at the missionary suspiciously. The white man's expression remained hard. With Rajendra's pride restored, he decided to stay and work. The harder he worked, the more willing he was to accept medical treatment and other things the missionary compound had to offer. Within months Rajendra's weak body recovered. He was strong, his skin was clean, his face was handsome, and his clothes fit him well. There was no resemblance to the filthy beggar that had almost died on Park Street.

One day a very beautiful and lovely creature entered Rajendra's world. He was on an errand far from Royd Street, and becoming hungry, had stopped at a tea stall to have a chapatta and a cup of tea. At another table across the dirt floor, he spotted an Indian girl dressed in western clothes. She was alone, quietly sipping her tea. She was beautiful. Rajendra knew he could live for weeks without ever seeing such a person again.

He was much too introverted to approach a woman, but he admired beauty. He looked carefully at the girl so he would remember her for his fantasies. Suddenly she looked up, her eyes caught his before he could turn away. At first he was shamed and embarrassed, but then he decided he had every right to look into her face. She flashed a charming smile. Rajendra's heart rocked.

Her face haunted him for days. He remembered her eyes. Many girls had been the subject of his fantasies, but never had he been struck by this kind of magic. There seemed to have been real communication. It was as though he knew her. He felt he was attractive to her, though that was impossible.

Often Rajendra would take the long trek across Calcutta to stop at the tea stall. He would wait patiently for his imaginary lover. She never appeared. He would carefully watch the people who passed by in the street, but he never saw her.

He was almost ready to give up when his patience paid off. One late evening she entered the tea stall. She was far more beautiful and elegant than he had remembered. The way she walked, her slim figure, everything about her filled him with pleasure.

She sat at the table next to him. Overcome with fear, his whole body seemed to freeze. Eventually, he began to relax and wished time could remain suspended. When she wasn't watching, he studied her. Her complexion was as smooth as cream. He was intrigued by her lipstick and painted nails, though before they had always seemed absurd to him. Everything about her was beautiful to him, even her western ways.

Rajendra could not let her know he admired her. It might make her angry. He began to feel uncomfortable and decided to leave. After he had paid for his food, he walked slowly out of the tea stall and into the street. He felt a strange sensation as though someone was staring at him. He turned suddenly; his eyes caught hers, the eyes that had enchanted him for days. She turned away quickly.

Rajendra rushed down the street delirious with excitement. He was sorry that he had embarrassed her, but he was intrigued. *She was staring at me. Why? Does she feel what I have been feeling? Surely not. But why was she staring at me? Perhaps it is all a coincidence.*

The next night Rajendra returned. He did not really expect her to appear. He had waited weeks for his second look at her. But fifteen minutes after Rajendra arrived, his mysterious lover walked in. Once again Rajendra's heart rocked. Once again she seemed more beautiful than the pictures his mind had kept of her. She was wearing the same clothes. That was good, perhaps she was not very rich even though the clothes looked clean and new. They fit her tightly and he noticed that her slacks were cuffed bell bottoms. Though ignorant of fashion, he guessed she was dressed according to the latest styles.

There were not many exchanged glances that night, yet there was a strange communication between the reluctant lovers. The next night they returned, and the next, too. No word was ever spoken. Rajendra feared that she would come with another friend, but she always came alone. They sat at different tables, each intrigued by the other.

One night the silence was broken. "I'm Bijoya. May I sit down?"

Rajendra stared, too surprised to speak. He had not prepared himself for this moment. At times he had wondered if she felt some attraction to him. Once he had arrived late, and she was there looking about nervously as though she were worried about him, but Rajendra could not bring himself to believe it was possible. He was sure that if they ever spoke it would be over. Once she knew of his life, she would not want to be near him.

That night was almost a dream. Conversation came easily. It was not at all what he had imagined. She was full of life; she poured out her problems to him. She thought herself weak and vulnerable, but Rajendra was terrified by her beauty.

"You are so strong and silent," she said. "You don't need anybody. I know. I've watched you. I wish I could be like you."

Rajendra was astonished.

"My father is a lot like you. Of course you're younger, but the same type." Bijoya grabbed Rajendra's hand excitedly. "You know the first time I saw you, I had just been to a Humphrey Bogart movie. You looked at me mean. But it didn't scare me. I thought you looked just like him." She laughed very softly.

Rajendra smiled. *Who is Humphrey Bogart,* he thought. He could not believe that she had touched his hand. It was so western. His mother would never have been so aggressive. *No woman has ever touched me like that.* Rajendra couldn't hear all that she was saying, because he was staring longingly into her eyes and filling his nostrils with the smell of her perfume.

He thought at any moment he would awaken, but he did not. Her voice sang to him, and Rajendra's voice began to sing too. He had never talked so much in his life. He could not believe his own ears as he heard himself spin tales of life in Cairo and his army exploits.

Rajendra raced through the streets that night. He remembered the jealous eyes of every man in the room as he walked her to the street.

Fear swept over him, a terrible fear. *She will discover that I live on the street, that I do not even have one room or even a roof. Perhaps I should not go back again. No, whatever happens, I must see her again.*

The following night it rained in Calcutta. The little tea stall was filled with people. Bijoya and Rajendra were packed tightly into the corner as with words and gestures they explored for common ground, expressing delight in each discovery.

At times Rajendra felt uneasy. The weaknesses in his personality, which he so despised, held a curious attraction for her. It seemed as though the very words which he feared would sound too hard, comforted her. When he would withdraw from her, she only pursued him more. Rajendra felt uncomfortable being close to someone so beautiful.

Before the night was over, the owner of the tea stall angrily threw everyone out. "There's no room for the customers. Get out, get out."

Bijoya and Rajendra, who had long ago finished their tea, were herded out into the street with the others. They tried to lean back under part of the tin roof, but the crowd pushed them out. Bijoya laughed, the rain poured all over her hair and clothes. They wandered down the street, close to the buildings to avoid the torrents of rain. They stopped under the edge of the thin roofing of a one-room shack. Bijoya leaned back into Rajendra's body to escape the downpour. They were silent.

Bijoya seemed to tremble. Rajendra kissed her wet hair, and the sweet smell of her perfume gave him a lonely sad feeling. He knew he would never know her as a woman.

"Here." She took his hand and put in it a piece of paper. He thought for a moment that she was crying, but maybe it was only the rain. She kissed him on the cheek and then ran down the street, disappearing into the night. As far as he knew, it was the only kiss anyone had ever given him.

Rajendra looked at the paper. It was a picture, not a good picture, but it was Bijoya.

Hours later Rajendra curled up on the street to try to sleep. Ordinarily the rain did not make him angry, but now he feared that it would ruin his picture of Bijoya. He would doze for a while, and then would awaken and run down the street until he found a small fire burning. He would pull out the picture of Bijoya and look at it in the light. A warm sensation would rush over him, and he would return to his niche in the wall to sleep.

The next day was difficult. Rajendra was tired, and he was worried. He had promised Bijoya that he would meet her parents. Rajendra felt conspicuous with her. Even when they were alone in the rain, he felt that people were watching, wondering why such a girl was with that man. Her parents would see how absurd it all was. They would ask questions. Rajendra felt sick.

Bijoya was waiting for him on the street outside the tea stall. She was wearing a western skirt. *She has other clothes,* he thought. *Perhaps her parents are more wealthy than I imagined.* He only casually glanced at her. It embarrassed him, but at the same time it amused him to see how the other men were eyeing her.

"Let's hurry, I can't wait for you to meet them."

They walked three blocks to a two-story stone building. Rajendra wanted to let Bijoya precede him up the stairs; he wanted to watch her beauty. But she must not know he had such feelings. Rajendra rushed on by her. Bijoya followed him up the stairs.

The family was waiting in the room. There were five or six people.

"Where do you work?"

"I am working on Royd Street now."

"How much do they pay you?"

"Two rupees a day." Rajendra had almost lied, but he could not.

"Where do you live?"

"I am staying on Park Street."

"You live on the street?"

There was a terrible silence.

Bijoya's father had no expression. His face was blank, "I want you to leave. Now. I never want you to see my daughter again."

Rajendra swallowed hard. He could see Bijoya out of the corner of his eye. He did not turn to look at her face, but rushed out and down the stairs quickly. His mind flashed back to Madras. He could see clearly the narrow street outside his mother's apartment.

Faster, faster, he moved. He did not run, but he moved swiftly with long strides. Something within him wanted to stop and turn. Perhaps she was following him. At this very moment she might be crying out. He could not take that chance. He was afraid. He dare not turn back, because if she was not running behind him, he knew he would kill himself.

In the early morning hours, Rajendra lay wide awake on the sidewalk. A sharp knife lay at his side. Once again he looked at her picture; once again a sensation of nausea overwhelmed him. Over and over he recounted the story—each gesture, each word from the very beginning. He could see her face clearly. He could taste her hair, wet with the rain.

He ran his fingers down the side of the knife blade. It was the only thing he had ever stolen. Rajendra did not feel guilty; he felt brave. He would not cut his wrists; instead, he would push the knife deep within his own stomach. It would take great nerve, and it would take great strength.

The old pye-dog, resting next to him, began to whine louder and louder, as though he had some God-given extra sense, as though he knew what was about to happen. He was an old friend to Rajendra. Theirs was a very independent relationship. They did not belong to each other, and they did not ask questions when one of them disappeared for a few days. Yet ever since he had returned to Calcutta, Rajendra and the old dog had been bumping into each other. There were thousands of brown mongrels roaming the streets, and there were thousands of beggars, but these two had a way of finding each other.

Rajendra's body felt numb all over. He dropped his knife. He lay sprawled out on the street exhausted. He was tired, too tired even to kill himself.

# 8

Before the sun came up, Rajendra went to work. He couldn't have told why. Perhaps his respect for work prevented him from even taking time off to die. Suicide was a personal affair; a job was something more. Even in the face of death it commanded reverence.

Several hours after the digging had begun, Rajendra heard his name called across the mission compound. "The pastor wants to see you."

The white man was seated at his desk, his face in his hands. When Rajendra appeared, he straightened up and smiled, but it did not conceal his anxiety. His eyes were bloodshot, his desk was stacked with letters, he looked harassed and tired.

The telephone rang. He answered it, listened, then asked for his calls and appointments to be held for him until later. As he firmly replaced the receiver, he looked at Rajendra. He sighed deeply, buried his face in his hands again, and groaned. It was a long, slow, agonizing groan. Rajendra stared at him. He thought the groan would never end. It seemed to come from somewhere very deep within the man, and Rajendra could feel it himself.

"Rajendra, Rajendra." The white man rubbed his face. His mind was returning from wherever it had been. "Last night I couldn't sleep. I saw you. You looked just as you did the afternoon we found you. You looked terrible."

The white man stared intently at him. Rajendra could not stand it; he looked away.

"I couldn't get you out of my mind. You had sores all over your body. You smelled. Do you know that you smelled so bad the day we found you that Bimal vomited when we took the rags off you? Several times while we bathed you, I thought you had died. I saw it all over again last night."

Rajendra shifted nervously in his chair. The missionary pointed his finger at him. "Rajendra, you still have those rags on. They are deep inside you, the same rags. I can't take them off you. Neither can you. Only Jesus can take those rags off you."

The white man buried his face in his hands again. He began to sob. His whole body shook violently as he wept. Rajendra sat for almost five minutes. The white man blew his nose and stood up. He walked to the door and stared out through the distorted glass window. "I didn't save your life."

The white man rubbed the glass window. His mind was far away again. "If it were up to me I wouldn't be here." It was as though he were all alone in the room. Rajendra had never seen him so tired.

Suddenly the missionary whirled; he leaned over the desk, using both hands to support himself. "Jesus saved your life. He did it, not me. Jesus loves you. I love you. Maybe your parents and brothers and sisters do too."

Rajendra was silent.

"But we can hurt you. Every person you have ever met will hurt you some day. They will walk right by you for a rupee, but not Jesus. Not Jesus, Rajendra. Jesus loves you. Jesus will never fail. It was Jesus who picked you out of the street and saved your life."

Rajendra swallowed hard.

"The men tell me you are good with statistics, you know your algebra well. I think I can get you in to take a test. I am going to try to get you a job as an accountant. It will pay you well. It will get you out of the ditches. You will be able to rent a room."

Rajendra was silent. He no longer cared.

"Someday, when we build our great hospital, we will need many, many accountants." He stared out the window as though visualizing that day way off. "These books from the library will help refresh your memory. One is a book on accounting. Study them. When you are ready, I'll see that you get a chance to take the test."

The heavy books plopped on Rajendra's lap. He glanced down at them. His face turned suddenly white, he looked stunned. Then Rajendra seemed to explode inside. His whole body began to shake violently. He had not cried since the day in Madras when he had run

*Three boys wait for food at the mission. The smallest has lost part of his hair due to malnutrition.*

*A nurse at the Christian Mission Hospital holds a baby who is being treated for head boils.*

starving to his mother's apartment. But he cried now.

The missionary turned and saw him, astonished that an act of kindness could be so meaningful. He had thought Rajendra resented him, a young man so hard nothing could break him. If he had known, he would have talked to him much sooner, but he had always been afraid it would drive him away. He patted Rajendra's shoulder.

"Thank you, Jesus," he murmured.

But the missionary did not really understand.

The big books had fallen to the floor—all except one. This one textbook Rajendra clutched tightly. Tears from his eyes splashed its pages. It was old and tattered, one the missionary had almost left in the library. *Maybe he will want to study algebra, too,* he decided. So he brought it along.

Rajendra felt the hard cover. He remembered lonely nights at St. Mary's when he had found comfort and companionship by studying the formulas from the book. His old friend had returned.

Long into the night Rajendra conversed with his friend. The algebra book had not changed; it still came right to the point, it probed and challenged. It asked questions, and Rajendra answered. He smiled; he was back in St. Mary's, and his heart was healed.

In the morning the wonder that continued to amaze Rajendra was not the book itself, but the way the book had come—right when he needed it. The words of the missionary stayed in his mind: Jesus loves you.

*Perhaps Jesus, whoever He is, does love me. But . . . have I the right to leave the ditches? Isn't my suffering for mistakes in a previous life? Isn't it best to remain patiently at work, would it be wrong to take the test?*

Rajendra picked up the old algebra textbook. It was after all only a book. He had thought the world would end when the sister had taken it away from him, but he had survived, he had gone to the army, the most splendid and satisfying years of his life. And the book had come back to him.

He thought of Bijoya. His world had not ended this time, either. *I shall not kill myself. I shall go on and take the test. I will leave the ditches, and I will become an accountant.*

Rajendra looked at the textbook. Some day Bijoya would come back, too. This time he would not be living on the streets. This time he will be ready for her.

Today Rajendra is an accountant. He wears a business suit, he sits in his office working until late, he lives in a two-room apartment. By western standards it is quite modest; yet compared to the streets, it is extravagant.

Fellow employees remark about his withdrawn personality. Some think he is conceited, others that he is a genius. Most speculate that something happened to him at an early age—though no one has ventured to ask what.

No one there knows his story, not even the white missionary. He agreed to tell me with these conditions: his name would be changed, the place and dates would be altered and the time sequences rearranged.

Rajendra is still waiting for Bijoya. He believes someone like her will step into his world. He is probably right.

Jesus is still the sahib's God. "I have seen Jesus," he said. "Hundreds of children line up in front of the church each morning and are served milk and parathas. That's when you see Him. As you watch the pastor with the children, you see Jesus in his face."

"I have also seen Jesus in my life. Twice God has saved me. He picked me out of the ditches, and He placed me here. I know that." He shrugged, "Perhaps some day I'll become a Christian."

There is a long pause. "If I do become a Christian, I will give up everything. Jesus taught that we must give our lives to Him. The Christians I know do not do that." Rajendra began to tap his desk with a pencil, "Except for the pastor. He is a Christian."

*Ram*

# 9

One evening in Calcutta, a white-haired old man walked slowly to his home. He was a proud old man with a stern look. He carried himself with dignity through the dirty streets, because he owned his own home. It was a fine two-room house which had taken many years and many bribes to purchase. It was crowded, and it had no toilet or running water, but it was a far cry from the squalor of the village where he had once lived.

Mr. Dutta's genius lay in securing an education for his children. He had accomplished this by professing Christianity. Some Christian schools had taken his sons at a reasonable price. Some, touched by the sight of fifteen people sprawling in a tiny mud hut, had agreed to teach them at no cost. Soon his children were all working, and Mr. Dutta had retired in relative wealth, supported by his boys.

His daughters had no jobs, but women were not important. "The role of the woman is to bear children for the husband," he often told his wife. "She should work the farm and make the clothes and cook the meals. Women can labor," he would add, "but decisions should be made by men. Old men, they are the most intelligent."

"You are very wise," his wife would answer.

One of Mr. Dutta's sons worried him. Ram's best grades had been in swimming. He had not secured a good job. A dreadful man hired him to load one-hundred-pound sacks of cement onto old wooden carts. After working from early morning to sunset, Ram received one rupee, less than a sweeper's wages. He was already fourteen years old, and though he gave every rupee to his father, his father paid all the food bills. Ram ate a lot—almost two meals every day. He had been working various hard-labor contracts since he was ten years old. Mr. Dutta had come to the conclusion that if Ram didn't do better soon, he must leave.

As the old man neared his home, he glanced down an alley. The sweet smell of opium engulfed him. For a moment he thought he saw his own son, but then began to feel guilty for suspecting such a thing. Just the same, he was an old man, and maybe he didn't know his son as well as he thought. He moved forward to investigate.

Ram was completely unprepared for the violence that suddenly descended on him. He was lying in a narcotic stupor when his father's hysterical voice shattered the air. The old man thrashed furiously with his cane. Ram's brothers heard their father's shrill old voice and rushed into the melee. Ram, braced against a wall while father and sons flayed away at him, was covered with blood when the boys finally stopped and pulled the old man off. Mr. Dutta was so beside himself they had been afraid he would have a stroke. He delivered one last hefty kick to Ram's groin. The boy groaned and collapsed.

Hours later, Ram crept furtively into his house to say farewell to his mother. She said nothing because her husband would demand a complete account of the conversation. She was afraid she might say something which would anger him. Ram understood. He knew his mother would tell him that she loved him if she could. They exchanged lonely glances. Then the boy left.

Actually Ram had been more enterprising than his father imagined. He had been earning much more than he gave his father. Big money, sometimes twenty-five rupees a week. His system was simple. After work he searched the streets for American soldiers. There were many in Calcutta en route to Viet Nam. Ram offered to find them prostitutes. The girls promptly rewarded him with a commission.

"Americans are funny," he often told his friends. "They never count their money. They just reach into a pocket, pull out a bill and say, 'Here, take it. Have yourself a ball.' Money means nothing to them, they are so rich. They don't realize they are giving us a day's wages."

Ram purchased a rail ticket to Delhi with his last forty-five rupees. He had no plans, he only knew he had to leave. Maybe his brother in Delhi could help him.

It hurt Ram because he really loved his father. He, too, had despised the squalid village, despised the filth and the opium dens. He wanted none of that life. There was something better for him.

His attitude had been blasphemy to the old Hindus in the village. They warned him that he couldn't change his destiny. He must be patient and in some future lifetime, he would be fulfilled. Ram refused to listen, and when the family had moved to Calcutta, he began to work for his better life.

He reflected his father's values, but seemed unable to meet his father's expectations. When the young Dutta could not earn enough rupees legally, he would do it other ways. But he could brag to no one of his success. To Mr. Dutta the boy was a failure. Ram, frustrated, had turned to drugs.

Mr. Dutta was getting older, and he had become impatient. "You are the black sheep of the family," old Dutta would screech at him. "Your brothers are not so stupid. They are not so lazy!" So Ram, a failure at fourteen, left home in disgrace.

The train ride to Delhi marked the turning point in his life. He was alone, strangely free, but overwhelmed with a desire to do something great. Greatness to a south Asian is likely to be the ability to accept his station in life with humility and pride. Ram's dream was much more western than that. He thought of the most extravagant thing he could. He dreamed of owning his own motor scooter!

With this intoxicating thought of luxury and power, the boy went to sleep. He was too naive to know he had been cut adrift in a sea of struggling humanity. He was only one of millions moving away from poverty and frustration. Sometimes, the move meant starvation and death. Cut off from his few contacts and opportunities, he had become prey to events.

Ram woke to a new companion, hunger. He had not realized how long it would take to reach Delhi. Asking around the train compartment, he was told two and a half days! At train stops he would wander across the platform. There was usually a man selling hot nuts. Ram would beg for some. Once he ate a leaf of cabbage which he pulled from a pile of garbage. He had deep stomach cramps which he would relieve by squatting at the edge of the platform to do his toilet. The train would whistle and he would be off again.

The train car was packed solid with human flesh, but each stop brought more people. They leaped onto the train even as it was moving, then they pushed and squeezed until everyone was in. At each stop the process was repeated until everyone was forced into a standing position. They were so tight that one single movement would cause a chain reaction throughout the car. Ram's arms pressed tighter to his body, and he was squeezed until he thought he would suffocate. When the car stopped the heat overwhelmed them and they were instantly wet with sweat.

By the time the train reached Delhi, Ram was in a daze. He stumbled from the train and collapsed on the platform. There he lay. He slept for two or three hours, then woke with spasms of hunger. He was too exhausted to reach out for help. There were others struggling about too. On a blanket a mother sat bewildered, her children screaming and pulling at her. Bold beggars moved in and out among the busy passengers.

It is hard to tell who really needs help in an Indian train station. Some are impostors, living comfortably because they look haggard or have a crooked leg; others look peacefully lazy but are actually dying. Ram was neither of these. He looked terrible. His face was infected and bruised from the beating his father and brothers had given him. He was burning with fever. These were not the theatrics of an imaginative beggar. Ram Dutta was for real.

On the fourth day Ram lost all appetite. The hunger cramps were over; starvation had set in. He had considered trying to reach his brother by telephone. But Ram did not know how a telephone worked, and he was much too proud to ask.

On the first day, one of the station employees had spotted him. He had watched him lying motionless hour after hour, watched him begging for help, watched him sip from puddles between the tracks. Finally he had seen him collapse on the platform. Even when the other beggars had looked him over for things to steal, he had not moved. He urinated right where he was, crumpled into a ball, retreating into the womb of death.

Ram had answered incoherently when the railroad employee questioned him, but the man had gathered he had a brother in Delhi who worked at a Goodyear factory.

"Pravesh," Ram mumbled over and over. "Pravesh will help me."

"Yes, yes," the employee had said, "but what is the rest of his name?" Then he listened patiently as Ram rambled on in his delirium, until he caught a name, Dutta.

A street-wise youngster had almost perished because he did not know how to operate a telephone. He survived. And in New Delhi his wildest dreams came true.

# 10

Ram Dutta stood before a large audience. He was pleased and surprised at his poise. Mr. Chester Bowles, the United States ambassador to India, was introducing him to the American personnel and their families.

"These four young men have been selected from more than six hundred applicants. They have been trained extensively in Bombay, and they are professionals. They are more than lifeguards. They have complete authority in the swimming pool area. Their word is to be obeyed."

Ram almost laughed aloud. He was thinking of his father who used to scream about his good grades in swimming. Ram was now earning more in a week than his father had ever earned in a year.

"Your life is in their hands," Chester Bowles said. "Let them help you."

Ram spotted a scowl on the face of several older women. Americans were funny. They didn't like to be touched by Indians. They thought they would catch a disease.

The young Americans were different. "Don't mix with the girls," Colonel Harper had warned him. "They are very fast. We want no scandals." Ram took his advice. But Indian girls were not off limits, and it was inevitable that Ram with his new position and money would eventually meet someone special. Success like misery needs company.

Ram met Premi at an embassy party. It was a glamorous night. Servants in tuxedos moved in and out among the guests with trays of cocktails. The tables were dripping with food. There was an orchestra playing, and all around them swirled the beautiful people of Delhi.

"I've seen you around. I'm Ram Dutta. I work at the American embassy."

"Premi." She held out her hand. No last name, just Premi. *Very western,* Ram thought. "I work in the British embassy."

"No wonder I've seen you around," Ram laughed. He had been hearing the American boys talk about her, but he was surprised by her beauty.

Ram and Premi spent the whole evening in animated conversation. He was soon in her spell. "Americans are simple to understand," she said with a laugh. "The young men all want drugs, the young women all want sex."

Ram smiled, "The Americans think they know so much about India. They know nothing. They do not understand."

"Why all of this preoccupation with drugs and sex?" Premi asked.

"What's involved is marijuana and hashish." Ram expanded his theory. "Drugs are something new to American youth. In their country they associate drugs with sexual permissiveness and rebellion. They assume since we are so knowledgeable and experienced with drugs, we are sexually permissive and anti-government as well."

"They are wrong," Premi looked carefully at Ram.

"Of course, they are wrong! Look at me. I work with them all day long. I am about as westernized as an Indian can become, but I would never bed one of those American girls. A man should only have intercourse with a prostitute or his wife."

"It is the way it has always been," Premi said, deciding from his language that Ram was indeed westernized.

"It is natural!" Ram continued. "It is the only natural way. The girl I marry will be a virgin."

"I will not marry for a long time," Premi said. "I do not want just any kind of life."

Ram's heart sank, but he did not resent her philosophy for it was his own. "I will not either. I will not marry until I have land, and a home, and complete security. I will not give all of this up."

They glanced around the elegant ballroom floor. *I agree with you Ram Dutta,* Premi said to herself. *You may not know it, but you and I are going to have quite a life together.*

Premi and Ram became a favorite couple to many in New Delhi's diplomatic circle. They danced from one embassy party to the next as though they were partners in an extravagant dream. Openly, they patronized their western friends; they smiled at their jokes and spoke to them in their "groovy slang." Secretly, they laughed at them.

"Westerners are soft. They are corrupted by all their wealth. They could never survive in India, and we will probably live to see them fail in the West too." They admired western industrialization and were infected by western materialism, but despised their youthful counterparts. They were proud of their great and ancient civilization. The hippies who began to descend on India claiming to study her religions, infuriated and embarrassed them.

As the months passed, Ram and Premi became more intimate in their love for each other. In the minds of some Indians, their unsupervised courtship was very western, but neither of them could abandon their sexual idealism. *A man only has intercourse with his wife or a prostitute,* Ram kept saying to himself.

One night Ram and Premi drifted away from the party. They strolled alone through the embassy gardens, talking about their work. But their minds were on each other. As they walked, their bodies would touch accidentally. The collisions were short and soft, but Ram was aware of them. He stopped and took Premi's hand. It was an important gesture. Indian motion pictures, violently conservative by western standards, sometimes end with the lovers grasping hands passionately.

The two lovers fell into their roles. This was India, so their love was confined to the touch of their hands, but as they touched, they both had second thoughts about their secret vow not to get married until they could afford it. In India that can be a long wait.

"What's it like?" Premi asked.

Ram shrugged without a comment. Western youth culture was having its influence. A few months ago she would never have ventured such a question.

Ram's mind wandered to thoughts about prostitutes. He thought about large filthy rooms with tiny cots, separated by portable wood and paper dividers.

*Sex will be much better with Premi,* Ram thought. *Marriage will be wonderful. We must wait though. We must wait. Marriage would ruin everything now.*

So the two lovers waited. Their inhibited need of sex manifested itself in a dozen ways. Ram returned to his drugs. There were violent arguments followed by weeks of silence. At times they hated each other as intensely as they had loved. Then in a tender moment, they would once again recite their vows of love.

Ram's opium habit increased sharply. For a year and a half, most of his money had been spent on drugs. They were always available. His friend Anwar Hugue had seen to that.

During these years, the motion pictures shown each evening at the American embassy were an occasional treat. One night Ram arrived late. Premi was standing on the steps of the large, modern, American building. Ram asked Anwar to let him off at the gate. Premi hated Anwar without being able to explain why even to herself. Ram thought it best to walk alone to the embassy door. If she did not see that he had been with Anwar, all the better.

"You're late!" she snapped.

Ram thought she was beautiful even if she was furious.

"Do you know what it's like to stand here while all our friends walk by me? Everyone asks, 'What's wrong?'"

"I'm sorry."

"What am I supposed to say to them?" She stalked back and forth.

"It couldn't be helped."

"I stood here for two hours! The movie is nearly over."

"Premi, my cycle broke down."

"Don't lie! Don't lie. I'm tired of this. I can't believe anything you say."

"I don't know what you're talking about." Ram didn't like the menacing tone in her voice.

"Ram, we made promises to each other. We've been working hard. I have been saving all my money. What's been happening to you?"

He could only shrug, "I don't know. I can't explain it."

"I can," she seemed near an explosion.

Ram stepped back so that the lights from the embassy could not catch the expression on his face. He loved Premi. She was the only one in his life who really mattered. He hated drugs—he hated himself. "Ram, will you tell me something? No lies?"

"Yes," he swallowed hard. "No lies."

Premi could not seem to find the words. "Do you love someone besides me?"

"No!" A sense of relief overwhelmed Ram. She did not know. She was so naive, of course she did not know.

"I mean, I don't mind the prostitutes," she was sniffling now. "I am glad there are prostitutes, or I'd think you were a fag like the American boys. And Anwar gives me the creeps."

Ram laughed at hearing such outrageous western slang from her. She laughed lightly too.

"There is no other girl. I love you. More than anything on earth, I love you. You are the only one I love," Ram whispered. But Ram knew that there was another mistress. One who was demanding his life.

Ram thought about Anwar Hugue and their plans for tomorrow night. He wondered if he would really go through with it. He wondered what drove him to risk his life for a drug experience. He wondered if he would ever see Premi again.

Premi was wiping the tears from her eyes. She smiled at him.

*Oh, God, don't let me do it,* Ram thought. He grabbed her hand and dashed across the embassy grounds. They stepped into the back of the room and watched the last hour of Rodgers and Hammerstein's *Oklahoma.*

# 11

Ram Dutta shuddered when he thought of his friend and their plans for the night. It had taken him a long time to decide. At first it had sounded hideous, but one night while he had been stoned on acid Anwar Hugue had described it in detail. The picture he painted had haunted Ram Dutta for days. He knew he would try it.

Their cycle sped through the back streets of Old Delhi, they curved and curved until Ram lost all sense of direction. Suddenly the cycle screeched to a stop. They waited. Out of the darkness a coolie appeared. He was pulling a ricksha. Anwar Hugue and Dutta got into the ricksha. Soon they were being hustled down a narrow alleyway, turning to the right and then to the left, deeper and deeper into a strange and hostile darkness. Ram Dutta settled back and cursed his stupidity.

The coolie stopped. A door in the wall opened. The coolie seemed to evaporate and the two young men stepped through the door into a large darkness. They could hear the echo of their own footsteps and the squealing and scurrying of rats. They kept stumbling forward, bumping into boxes and occasionally splashing in water. Eventually Ram spotted the flicker of a candle. As he reached it, the candle began to move. The boys followed, occasionally catching glimpses of a large figure ahead of them. A door swung open.

"There he is!" Anwar whispered excitedly.

In a tiny room lit by a gas lantern, Ram saw an old Indian snake charmer wearing only a loin cloth and a turban. His face was tired and wrinkled. He sat cross-legged before a basket.

"Sit down." The old man's voice was soft, barely audible. Ram noticed that his eyes were closed. Anwar Hugue and Dutta sat down on a mud floor. The door clanged shut behind them, and they heard a bolt slip into place. Ram Dutta's heart began to beat rapidly.

"Do exactly as I say," the old man whispered. "You were not followed?"

"No," Anwar Hugue said.

"Do you understand that this could kill you?"

"Yes," Ram said, "I am ready. I have paid. This is what I want."

Anwar had told him this was the ultimate drug experience. The snake had already received an injection of opium. The potency of the narcotic increased as it moved through its system. The old charmer lit a cigarette. His eyes were still closed. He partially lifted the lid from the basket and blew a puff of smoke into it. Anwar Hugue began to edge away to the corner of the room, but he motioned Ram to stay where he was.

"Here." The old man blindly extended his hand with the lit cigarette.

Anwar motioned to Ram to take it. Ram positioned himself in front of the basket opposite the snake charmer and took the cigarette.

"Puff smoke into the basket. Wiggle your tongue afterward so that he can see."

Ram looked into the top of the basket and saw the head of the snake. His heart began to pound again.

"Puff!" The old man said.

Ram took a drag and blew into the snake's face. The snake squirmed and struggled. The old charmer placed his hands on the side of the basket as if to read the snake's reaction.

"Puff!" The snake charmer now spoke loudly and clearly.

Ram repeated the process.

"Puff!"

Now the snake was thrashing about wildly.

"Puff!" The old man's eyes were still closed but with his hands he was sensing the fury of the snake.

"Puff!"

Once more Ram blew the smoke. His heart was beating like a bass drum.

"Now!" The old man screamed it! His eyes opened. They were wild with terror. In an instant the snake leaped from the basket and bit deeply into Ram's tongue. Ram's mouth and nose were smashed by the impact. He was knocked flat. It happened in a second. Before the old man had finished saying "now," Ram Dutta was unconscious.

The others, except for Anwar, left immediately, taking the lantern with them. Anwar stayed with him through the night, sleeping uneasily, occasionally slapping the rats who sniffed around Ram's still form. By morning a ray of light penetrated into the large adjacent room and Ram awakened.

"Am I alive?" He could hardly talk. His tongue was so swollen that it almost choked him.

"You're alive." Anwar pulled him up. "Let's get out of here."

Ram was numb. He rubbed his face, but felt nothing. "I cannot move," he said and fell back down.

"I am getting out of here." Anwar Hugue scrambled for the door. "There are rats all over this place." He turned back to Ram, "Come on!" Then he too disappeared.

Ram Dutta lay alone in the darkness. *Oh, Vishnu, if I ever recover I shall not be so stupid again. Let me live.*

He closed his eyes, but instead of the great Hindu god Vishnu he saw the terrifying image of Shiva the destroyer, the god of war, famine, and death. Ram opened his eyes quickly, but the terror remained. Shiva had extended his bowl made of a human skull. The bowl was crawling with snakes.

"Vishnu!" Ram's voice shattered the darkness. "Vishnu! Help me." But he could only see Shiva. When his eyes closed, even in a blink, he saw the terrifying image.

Ram shut his eyes and studied the evil image. It was Shiva's figure all right. It was Shiva's costume. It was his bowl and snakes. But the face, the face was not Shiva's. It was Ram's father.

"Father!" He cried out in horror. "Forgive me, Father! Do not destroy me, Father. Take away your curse!"

# 12

"Ram?"

The voice awakened him to darkness.

"Ram!"

The voice again. It was Anwar Hugue stumbling through the adjacent room. He had come back. Ram sat up. Several rats scurried away from him. He felt his face. It was numb. There was water on his fingers. As his swollen tongue touched his finger tips, he knew that it was not water at all, but blood.

"Ram!" Anwar was closer, feeling for the door. Ram tried to answer but he could not.

He licked at the blood on his fingers. Rats, he thought. Then he vaguely remembered the long struggle drifting somewhere between semiconsciousness and total darkness. He had brushed at the rats, but they had not been intimidated by his hands, sensing he was no threat they had bitten him.

"I am here!" Ram managed to say. His head began to pound as he spoke.

The door swung open and a gas lantern filled the room with light. Anwar Hugue gasped as he saw the rats disappear into the floor and walls. One moment they had covered the floor like a carpet, the next they were gone. Ram's eyes shut involuntarily at the brightness of the lantern.

Anwar stooped next to him. "There's a man who wants to see you. Ram, come on. You can't stay here."

Hugue lifted him to his feet, and they stumbled out the door and into a waiting ricksha. It was dark outside. Ram had come to this place two nights ago; it seemed like an eternity.

"We're going to my place," Hugue said. "I'll clean you up. Then you've got to meet a man. Maybe he has a job for you—the embassy called to say you're fired." Hugue laughed.

It took too much effort to say out loud, but Ram was hungry and was glad of it—glad to be alive and glad to feel hungry.

"You'll have to get some shots for those bites," Hugue said. "This man waiting for you, he says he's got to talk to you."

The ricksha clacked through the silent streets past hundreds of sleeping people circled on the sidewalks. Occasionally there was a yellow light burning from a low watt bulb. Sometimes a dog would sniff at the heels of the coolie. Ram's senses were returning. He knew he would live.

Michael Jordon was one of the biggest men Ram had ever seen. Ram had been told to look for a black man, that was all. When he stepped into the lobby of the Imperial Hotel, Jordon loomed before him. "I'm Michael Jordon." His teeth flashed; he extended his right hand toward Ram as though to say, "Give me five, baby."

Ram considered momentarily that it was some kind of test. "Ram Dutta." He slapped Jordon's hand in the greeting of American blacks.

"Let's grab something to eat." The big black man turned and walked through the lobby. Ram followed. Everyone in the room seemed to be looking at him.

How did he recognize me? Ram thought. He glanced at the enormous Afro hair style and suddenly realized that he did not know anything about black men. I wonder what he wants?

They sat in the open sunshine in the garden patio. Several workers were squatted on the grass. They were hunting for weeds, as rare as four-leaf clovers in the beautiful lawn. A wall of palm trees and exotic flora separated the garden from the shacks on the other side.

Jordon scowled at the menu, "What do you want?"

"Oh, nothing," Ram was nervous.

A young Indian waiter appeared wearing a freshly starched uniform.

"I'll have this Neapolitan pizza," the black man said. Then he exploded with laughter. "Pizza!" he shouted. Then he laughed until tears rolled from the corners of his eyes.

The waiter stood patiently. "Is there anything else?"

"Make it two pizzas," Jordon said. "And two glasses of this wine."

"Yes sir." The young waiter left them.

Ram spoke carefully. "It must be strange for you to travel all the way to India and find pizza on the menu."

Jordon eyed him suspiciously. "What makes you think I have traveled a long way? How do you know where I come from?"

Ram wondered why the black man frightened him. "I just assumed you came a long way. I don't know."

"Well, that's not hard to figure," Jordon sneered, "I'm from Toronto."

"Canada?"

"Yeah, Canada," Jordon answered. He pulled out a package and slapped it on the table. Ram's head spun in all directions to see if anyone was watching. The servants attending the lawn were far away. The waiters were in the adjacent dining area. Ram could feel their eyes watching through the window shades. On the table was a package of hashish. The black man stared at Ram silently.

Ram thought fast. He glanced once more around him, pulled a package from his belt, and slapped it down on top of the other. Jordon's eyes opened wide. "Aha!" he said. Once more he exploded with laughter, a tremendous roar which seemed to shake the ground. Inside Ram was nervous. He wanted to grab both packages of hashish and hide them quickly. He was sure that he was being watched, and he wanted to warn the black man not to be so loud. Outwardly he remained calm.

The black man shook so hard that his chair creaked and shifted under his weight. The black man's convulsions of laughter finally ran their course, then he stared silently. Ram did not avoid the black man's eyes.

"I know all about you, Ram Dutta." Ram did not reply.

"I have friends in the American embassy. You've helped a lot of my friends get junk. What would you say if I told you that I came all the way from Canada just to meet you?"

"I wouldn't believe you."

Jordon's face changed in a flash. His muscles flexed, and he growled with anger. "Well, that's exactly what I did! You better damn well believe it."

Ram was frightened, but he tried desperately not to let it show. "What do you want?"

"I want you to work for me."

"But I already have a job."

"You're finished. The embassy fired you! Look man, don't get smart with me. I said I know everything about you. Everything!"

"I've a friend who can get me a job at a hotel."

Jordon ignored him, "I pay a hundred dollars a day."

Ram flinched. "I don't believe it."

"I don't care whether you believe it or not. All I want you to do is say you'll work."

"What do you want me to do?"

"I want you to get me junk."

"A hundred dollars a day is a lot of money."

"I want lots of junk! I want every kind of drug you've ever heard of. I want to know how you take it. I want movies of you. I want you rolling it, and smoking it, and shooting it. I want you to help me find out where it all comes from. We'll go to Bombay, we'll go to Calcutta. And I'm paying!"

The young waiter appeared at the door of the dining room, carrying a large tray. They watched the waiter make the long march across the patio and on to the lawn.

"Pizza Neapolitan," the young man announced. He forced a smile and awkwardly served the small pizzas. The waiter's hands shook as he poured the Indian wine. Jordon sniffed his glass. "Oh," he growled disgustedly.

The waiter nodded apologetically, "You do not want it?"

"Oh, that's all right," he waved him away. "Go on, go on!"

The servant stepped backwards and then retreated hurriedly with the empty tray.

"There's more," the black man said. He sipped his wine. Over the top of the glass his eyes bore in on Ram.

"What else?"

"I want you to go back to the snake charmer, and I want you to take me with you." Ram's head began to pound. "I want you to take another fix. I am going to watch. I want to see what it is like."

Outwardly Ram remained calm. Inwardly he was reacting violently. *No! I'll never do it again. Not for anybody. Not for money.* But it was useless. Ram knew he would go back. He had already considered it once, though he could not understand why. For a hundred dollars a day he would go back to the snake charmer, he would get junk for this man, he would teach him what he knew.

Michael Jordon lay a bundle of rupees on the table. Ram looked at it, but he did not move. Jordon pushed the money across the table. Ram Dutta nodded his head. He took the money and grabbed his package of hashish. The black man howled with laughter. Ram Dutta hated him.

Calcutta was hot. It was like living in an oven. Though Jordon and Dutta stayed at the Oberoi Grand, an elegant hotel with air conditioning and a great dining room, they didn't benefit much from its cool comfort. They were seldom there. From early morning until late at night they talked junk. They must have met with a hundred people: some were businessmen, some lived in the bustees. Ram was interpreter, guide, and adviser to Jordon. Finally one night they returned to the hotel early.

"Let's have a drink." Jordon ducked into the cocktail lounge. "I want you to pack my bags."

Ram almost did not hear his last remark. "Tonight? Are we leaving Calcutta?"

"Not we, I am leaving Calcutta," the black man said.

"Where are you going?"

The black man leaned back in a comfortable chair with a sigh, "Back to Canada."

"Tomorrow?"

"Tomorrow. You have my bags packed tonight."

Ram was surprised, "You'll want to take a lot of junk."

"No! No junk." The black man leaned over the small table. "I will take nothing with me." He smiled. "You will send it to me."

Ram didn't like the black man. He didn't like the way he ordered him around or the way he assumed things. Ram had never complained; a hundred dollars a day is a fortune. "Mr. Jordon," he shook his head, "I don't know if I can do that."

Jordon ignored him. "We have a network of suppliers all over west Bengal now. If you just do what you're told, you'll make a lot of money. You need help. Someone you can trust with your life, someone who's hooked like you, someone who needs lots of junk. In a few days some men will show up. They are going to tell you how to pack the stuff." The black man smiled big, "We put them in pickle jars."

Ram did not smile. "I don't want this!"

"Yes!" Michael Jordon shouted at him, "You want it. You need it. You have to have it!"

Ram turned to see if the others in the lounge were looking at them.

"I've seen a lot like you," the black man growled, "You need the junk and you need the money, too."

"Mr. Jordon," Ram spoke just above a whisper, "I hate it. I hate the junk! I've hated every minute of these last few weeks. In my village were some old milk men who always smoked the stuff. I hated those old men. I always told myself I'd never be like them."

"Get my bags packed," the black man said.

In spite of himself Ram was impressed. Jordon was so sure of himself. He had lots of money. He was so cocky. Why did he give Ram such great responsibility? Ram was convinced he could handle the job, but why was the black man so sure of him? Why did he trust him so quickly? It seemed a big risk. It made Ram think a lot about himself. *What does he see when he looks at me? Am I a drug addict? Is that what he thinks I am? That is what my father saw when he looked at me.*

For six months Ram Dutta ran the operations from Calcutta. He was restless and at times frightened. He remembered Jordon's advice and decided he needed a friend. One evening he made a rendezvous with an old boyhood pal. They were to meet in a tea stall near Ram's own home. Ram waited for almost an hour. Occasionally he felt like returning to his father's house. He wanted to see his mother and his brothers and sisters. He wanted to tell them about embassy parties and the great politicians he had talked to in New Delhi. He wanted to see his father's face when he pulled out his roll of bills. But he could not go home. His father would say he was still a drug addict. He would not go home. Not yet.

Finally Ashoke arrived, "Ram, I didn't recognize you at first. I am so surprised to see you. What's this all about?"

"Sit down." Ram looked around him, "You didn't tell my father?"

Ashoke was silent for a moment. "Ram, your father died a year ago." There were several minutes before either spoke. "I'm sorry," Ashoke said.

Ram played with his teacup. Then suddenly his mood changed. "Ashoke, I am so glad you are still here. A lot has happened to me. You wouldn't believe it all. I need your help badly. I am making big money, thousands of rupees. I have to stash it somewhere."

"Why don't you put it in the bank?"

"No, no, I can't do that. Listen," Ram whispered, "it's from junk."

"What do you want me to do?"

"I want you to help me. I'm running a big organization."

"Ram, I can't help you. I'm sorry. I can't do anything like that."

"You know what it means? It means any kind of stuff you want. Free. As much as you want."

"No, you don't understand. I'll help you in any way I can, but not with the drugs."

"You have to!" Ram shot back. "You need it! You have to have it. You need junk like the rest of us."

Ashoke returned quietly, "No, Ram, you're wrong. I don't need junk. I haven't even smoked grass for years."

Ram Dutta was stunned. He fumbled with his teacup. How was it possible for someone to play around with opium and leave it so easily? What kind of life did Ashoke have without grass? "What's happened to you? What kind of life do you live?"

Ashoke hesitated, "I'm a Christian."

"Oh," Ram threw his hands up in the air, "So you're a Christian. That shouldn't matter. I have known Christians. You aren't going to try to tell me they won't even let you smoke grass!"

"Look, Ram, I went to the shacks. Remember, the old shacks where we smoked stiel? Well, I went there for years. Every night I would get off work and go to the shacks. We all did. All your old friends in the neighborhood. I got to where I didn't like it, but I couldn't quit, you know?"

"Of course. You can't quit junk."

"Well, there's a place on Royd street, a church. Some people I knew went there, so I went too. They had good music. I kept going. One day I told the pastor about the stuff I was taking. He and some other men prayed. Then this strange thing happened." Ashoke took a sip of his tea. "Well, I've never taken junk since."

Ram sat for a very long time staring at Ashoke. "I don't believe you," he finally said.

"It's true. It's true. Listen Ram, this pastor is like a prophet. He's always praying, even when he talks he is praying in between. He is sort of like a specialist. He has people waiting to see him all the time. He gives away food. He finds work for people."

Ram glared back at Ashoke. "You won't help me?"

Ashoke tapped the table, "Sometimes I think it would be great to go to the shacks, just to have a joint or two."

Ram pressed him, "There's a lot of money in this."

Ashoke shook his head. "I can't. I just can't do it."

"Thanks," Ram sneered.

"He's a white man," Ashoke said.

"Who?"

"The pastor." Ashoke smiled. "There are always children following him around."

"So, why are you a Christian?" Ram asked.

"Well, I hated the drugs. I liked them, and I hated them too. When I needed the drugs, I just prayed to Jesus. I just kept saying 'Jesus,' like the pastor. I feel so good now. I am working, and I am studying the Bible."

"You read the Bible?"

"Yeah, sure."

"Luke and Matthew?" Ram smiled at the odd sound of the names. They were familiar to him from his early days at the Catholic school, yet it seemed so strange to think that his old friend was into that sort of thing.

They both laughed.

"Corinthians," Ashoke said, and they laughed again, but Ram could not think of another book in the Bible to keep it going.

"I feel so strong and healthy." Ashoke took a deep breath. "That stuff always wore me out."

Ram looked at him. He did not speak, he just stared and thought. *I have been all over India. I have met the most important people in this country. I have earned more money than Ashoke will earn in all of his lifetime, but God, how I would like to trade places with him.*

"Ram, I might get married," Ashoke said.

*Premi,* Ram thought. *Premi.* He felt empty and lonely. He wanted her. He wanted to be free from junk. He wished that Jesus could help him. He wished the black man were wrong.

# 13

"Yes, come in." The pastor opened the door to his office. An electric fan was blowing, but even so the sahib was sweating. "Sit right here."

They both sat quietly. Eventually the white man looked at him, "Now, Ashoke tells me you have a drug problem."

"Yes."

The pastor jumped up from his chair. "Many, many drug addicts have come through this office." He looked at the young Indian. "Now, I want to ask you a question. I want the truth. Do you understand that?" Ram nodded. "No one has ever prayed for you as many prayers as I am going to pray in the next few weeks. Not even your mother. Some nights we won't sleep. Sometimes a group of men will pray all night long for you." Ram felt chills all over his body as the white man spoke.

"Once we start to fight this thing we aren't going to stop until we win. Do you understand that?" Ram nodded. "These streets are filled with drug addicts. We don't have enough room to handle them all. We have only a little house for drug addicts. So I have to ask you these questions, and I want the truth."

Ram nodded again.

"Do you really want to give these drugs up?"

Ram thought of a letter he had written to Michael Jordon, a letter that could cost him his life. "Sir, I have to. I have to!"

"Do you really hate drugs?"

"I hate them, sir. I hate them. They have destroyed me. I could have done many great things in life, but I have been a prisoner all these years."

The white man sat back in his seat. He looked exhausted. He groaned softly. He picked up the telephone. "Tell one of the associate pastors to come in here." He placed the receiver back and stared at his bookcase.

Ram followed the blade of the fan on the ceiling. It moved slowly, round and round. They waited in silence. "Pastor?" Ram broke the silence. The white man looked up. "Pastor, there is this girl; her name is Premi. She is the only good thing that has ever happened to me. I have earned lots of money and lost it all. That does not hurt me. But Premi, I don't know how to say this," Ram broke into sobs. He felt like a little child in the presence of this man. "Can Jesus give me back Premi?"

The sahib stood and walked around his desk. He leaned over until he was only inches from the Indian's face. "Oh, God," he said, "these damnable, damnable drugs." He gritted his teeth. "These damnable, damnable drugs." The pastor placed both hands on the Indian's head. "Oh, Jesus, precious Lamb of God, here is another one." The white man looked upwards as though God were right there. "Here is another one. You brought him here. You brought him here to save him."

Ram sobbed.

The door opened. One of the associate pastors, a handsome Indian, dressed impeccably, stepped in. The pastor looked at him. "Drugs," he said.

The associate nodded and patted Ram on the shoulder.

The white man squeezed his eyes tightly shut. "Now Satan, you have already begun to lose your power. We claim this man for Jesus!"

The associate pastor stood dignified. He kept his hand on the Indian's shoulder and prayed silently.

The telephone rang. The pastor leaned across his desk to answer it. "I've got to go," he said, "I've got to go."

"I'll pray with him," the associate said, waving the pastor out.

"Make sure that he comes to prayer tomorrow morning," the white man said as he disappeared out of the office.

Ram was frightened. At first he had been almost hypnotized by the pastor. He had persuaded himself that with mental concentration and a little Christian magic he could overcome the drugs. Now he revolted against the whole thing. It was too strange. He could only hope the Indian associate pastor would quickly end his prayer so he could get out of the place.

"We have a prayer meeting at five-thirty," the associate told him.

"Yes, I'll come," Ram said. He raced out the door and down the street.

*We've lost him,* the Indian pastor thought. *Something we said or did. We've lost him.* The associate pastor watched Ram Dutta disappear into the crowded Calcutta street. *We cannot help everybody,* he thought. *There are too many.* He sighed deeply and breathed a prayer. There would be many more drug addicts during the week. And orphans and refugees who needed help. There was, even then, a long line of people in the hall with horrible stories to tell. Someone must hear them, someone give them hope. Jesus had died for each one of them, but the mission couldn't help them all. There was not enough money. There was not enough time.

The Indian pastor walked across the compound to his office. He was content to run the school. It was a great responsibility. Yet more and more he felt responsibility slipping from the pastor's shoulders to his. He sat down at his desk. The disappointment over the young drug addict lingered. *Oh, God, bring him back to us again. Give us one more chance. Please, God, bring him back.*

Ram raced into the bustee. He had not been there since the visit with Michael Jordon. He found the old hut and groped into the darkness. He took a deep breath, inhaling the smoke with delight as though it were fresh air. He plopped to a floor crowded with bodies, rolled a joint of grass, and leaned back in comfort.

For one full day Ram lived in the old shack. But the nightmare of his predicament refused to be ignored. Memory of his letter to Michael Jordon, finally burst through his drugged euphoria and sobered him quickly. Eventually his money would run out. There would be no payments from Canada. Ram staggered out of the bustee and down the street toward his apartment. He had no sooner reached his neighborhood than the white man appeared.

Ram froze. *How did he find me? I did not leave my address. This is impossible.*

The white man crossed the street. "Ram?"

*How could he remember my name?*

The white man stood in front of him.

Ram took a deep breath. It was as though he had completed a long journey. "Pastor, I meant to thank you for your prayers."

"Ram, have you been taking drugs?"

"No, pastor." The white man only stared at him. "Yes, pastor. I have been smoking grass. It is not like opium."

The white man's eyes bore in on him. "Ram Dutta, Jesus Christ has set you free. You are no longer a drug addict."

Ram was nervous and anxious to leave. "Yes, pastor, thank you, thank you."

"Ram, I have a book I want you to read. It is the book of *John*. I want to show you this verse." The pastor read it slowly, "If therefore the Son shall make you free, you shall be free indeed."

"Yes, thank you, pastor. Thank you for the book." Ram darted down the street.

It almost seemed as though the young Indian had evaporated, he vanished so quickly in the people-choked street. The white man looked closely and finally spotted him. He was ten yards away walking at a fast pace through the crowds.

The missionary stood still; he glanced around him at all the people. Stacks of correspondence awaited him in his office. He mentally sorted through the dozens of emergency problems that needed his immediate decision. Then he glanced back down the crowded street toward the young Indian. Perhaps he should let him go. There were so many others.

The white man began to follow Ram's path, walking very slowly. There was no chance of catching the Indian. He was looking for something else. His eyes panned the street from gutter to gutter. Almost a block from where they had parted, he spotted what he was looking for—the *Gospel of John* which he had given Ram, lying in the dirt. He picked it up. The book opened easily to the verse he had read to Ram, "If therefore the Son shall make you free, you shall be free indeed." There was to be no work that afternoon. The great machinery at the mission compound would have to run itself. The pastor was going to pray.

At the mission compound in Calcutta the day begins at five-thirty each morning with a prayer meeting. The white man is always there. One morning Ram Dutta appeared at this meeting. He stood like a ghost in the doorway. The pastor stared at him, his Indian associate pastor struggled to remember.

"Pastor, will you help me?"

The white man reached for him and brought him to the center of the room.

"Gentlemen, this man wants deliverance from drugs," he announced. There were Indian businessmen in suits and workers who had stopped by to pray at the beginning of their day mingled together here. They surrounded Ram. They touched him on the shoulder, on the head, on the back. They touched him, and they prayed. There were loud exclamations of, "Praise the Lord," or "I rebuke you, Satan." Ram was desperate. He had expected something strange, but he had determined to stick it out and give it a chance to work. He gritted his teeth and waited.

The associate pastor stepped back from the crowd. Now he remembered the young Indian. He remembered how he'd been scared off last time. Perhaps he would be turned off again. Perhaps their ideas of prayer were too strange for him. *Oh God,* the associate pastor prayed, *let him find you in spite of us and all our noise.*

Ram struggled with himself. It felt crazy. These were intelligent people. How could they believe in this. *Oh God, if you are there, please help me. Please help me. Take away the drugs!*

One by one, each person in the room slipped away. Finally Ram sat in a chair across from the pastor. The white man only stared at him. Ram was exhausted. He leaned back and stretched, staring at the ceiling. Then he looked at the floor, "Pastor, is there really any hope for someone like me?"

The white man looked at him for a long time. "Ram Dutta," he said slowly, "you are a free man. The Spirit of God is all over you. Jesus is all over your face. You will never take drugs again."

In spite of himself, Ram laughed. He liked the pastor. He didn't understand him but he liked him. The pastor couldn't know how much money he had earned or how important he had been in New Delhi, yet the pastor always looked at him with great respect. Ram could see it in his eyes. Remembering, he says now, "The pastor never did think of me as a drug addict. I was always a free man to him. It felt good, if only for a few moments, to have someone believe in me."

The sahib put his arm around the young Indian. "Oh Jesus, thank you for this great victory. Thank you for Your saving power." Ram could see the face of Michael Jordon; he was laughing.

For two days Ram took nothing. At times the craving was not so great. He imagined a miraculous cure. But the Christians said, "Sometimes God gives a miracle and one simply stops, but usually it is cold turkey. That is why we want you to stay in our house." Ram wouldn't stay with the other addicts. He would fight this alone.

On the third day Ram's nerves were strained beyond endurance. He could not keep his food down. He raced out of his apartment and down the streets, deliriously happy with his decision: he would not take a strong drug, only mandrake. He could have chosen something much stronger, but he had the good sense to choose a mild opiate. It would help, at least psychologically. He was pleased with himself.

He found the shack and stumbled in. There was a circle of smokers sitting cross-legged. A stick was passed from one to the next without conversation. The circle widened for Ram. He sat and waited as the stick passed from one mouth to the next. It was very dark. Ram's eyes struggled to make the adjustment. When the stick reached him, he passed it on without a drag. He was suddenly curious, and he wanted to have a look around.

When the stick eventually came to him again, he paused and once more passed it on without a taste. Ram sighed deeply. *You may regret that,* he thought. *You may not be able to survive until it comes back to you again.* But when the stick once more reached his fingers, Ram was still relaxed. He passed it on. *Perhaps I am cured after all.*

He studied the faces. For the first time he saw people. Like him, they were mostly young men. But there was also an old man. He was wearing a turban. He had the stick now, sucking deeply, his old wrinkled face contorted. Each face revealed a world of its own. Ram was astonished. He had visited many shacks like this but he could not remember ever having looked at faces.

Ram leaned back out of the circle and followed the tiny glow of the stick as it moved round and round. The old man retreated to a corner of the room and fumbled with sticks and leaves and fire. He returned with another burning stick.

*I am free,* Ram thought. He looked at the others in surprise and bewilderment. *I am free. I am free!* He leaned against the wall of the shack and wept for joy.

Ram Dutta stayed for hours, watching the little glow circle the room. Each time the stick passed the place where he had been sitting, he would feel a strange sensation. Chills ran up and down his arms as he realized he did not want, did not need the narcotic. *You are free,* he thought, and his whole body shook.

Once Ram inhaled deeply to see if the odor would trigger desire, but there was no response. He thought about the future, about Premi. He decided that he must be very careful. He did not want to lose this freedom. He would return to the pastor. He would do willingly whatever he suggested, even if it meant moving into the house with the other addicts.

When Ram left the hut it was dark. He moved quickly through the bustee. The shacks and narrow alleyways eventually gave way to brick buildings and main streets. Ram was soon running. A clanging trolley car rushed down the street. As usual the car was full, but Ram jumped on, hanging to a handle on the side. Tears still ran down his cheeks.

The world seemed to come alive. As the trolley sped down the streets, he studied the faces of the people he passed. He saw the street vendors packing their wares, he saw the poor widows and orphans huddled under their rags. *It is wonderful to be free,* he thought. *I could have all the money in the world, and still be a prisoner.*

When Ram reached the compound, he was still bursting with joy. The large auditorium was filled with people. They were singing. Ram went in and sat for a moment, but he was too excited to sit. He went out and wandered into the courtyard. The white man had seen him come in and out again. As the service drew to a close, he appeared in the doorway. Ram saw him and smiled. "Pastor, you were right."

The two faced each other for a moment. The white man was not exactly sure what had happened to the young Indian. Ram was not sure himself and could not explain how he felt. Finally he just shouted aloud. It burst from him. Several nearby were startled, the crowd in the auditorium heard it, dozens of people passing by the gates of the compound heard it, and wondered what it meant. "I'm free!" Ram shouted.

The white man grinned hugely and shouted back as if to join in the celebration, "FREE!"

"Oh, pastor, you were right, I shall never take drugs again."

"And who did this for you, Ram?" The white man asked. "Who is more powerful than the drugs?"

"Oh, pastor, Jesus. It is Jesus."

The white man threw his arms around Ram. Bimal joined them in the courtyard. Soon others gathered too.

"Gentlemen," the pastor said, "Jesus has just delivered this man from drugs."

The little group responded by clapping. They clapped in joy and appreciation. There were not very many, but they clapped enthusiastically. They clapped and clapped, and they did not stop—as though by clapping a long time they could make up for their small number.

This attracted attention, of course. Bimal motioned to the curious people who gathered and told them to join the applause. They did, though they did not yet know why. Bimal moved in and out among this growing crowd, laughing and gesturing like a cheerleader lest the applause weaken. "Jesus never fails," he told them. "Jesus never fails!"

The pastor started applauding too. Even Ram, infected by this enthusiasm, clapped and laughed and cried with joy all at the same time.

Far above them, far above the light and noise of the great city of Calcutta, God sat and watched. God could hear the applause and the laughter, and He smiled.

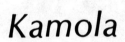

*Kamola*

# 14

Kamola Bala sat like a goddess in the ricksha. You'd never guess she was only sixteen. She looked at least twenty-five. She had elegance. It was not just her clothes, which though soiled were of the latest fashion. Mostly, it was poise. The kind of poise that comes from experience. She knew that she was beautiful, and she knew exactly what men looking at her thought.

The ricksha rolled through the streets of Calcutta, clacking over stone pavement, twisting and turning block after block. Occasionally, Kamola would shout a direction to the old driver, then sit back and return the glances of the men. Twice she recognized a face, but usually she had to guess at their professions and the kind of homes they came from.

The street narrowed, and soon the ricksha driver came to a halt. Kamola paid him handsomely. She walked across the railroad tracks and into the muddy street of a crowded slum.

She hadn't seen her old neighborhood in four years. No one recognized her. Women stood ringing their hands in the doorways and shouting to the men, who watched Kamola pass and shot mischievous looks at each other. Trash heaps yielded up hordes of dogs barking and yelping at the defiant intruder.

For a moment Kamola hesitated. She glanced down the street. Smoke from the little fires seemed to hang like clouds over the whole neighborhood. From a little tin shack streamed a trail of smoke. Her parents were home.

"Child, I knew you would come." The old woman grabbed her daughter.

Kamola let out a gasp. Her mother's rags hung on her body, her

111

hair was tossed and tangled, she had no teeth.

"Where is father?"

The old woman shrugged. "He has been gone. He left when you left."

Kamola stared at her in disbelief. She had long since learned to doubt her mother.

"He has been gone, I tell you. He left us. I have not seen him in four years. I have done everything myself." The woman returned to a pot burning on a little fire.

Kamola's eyes began to adjust to the room. She saw her brothers and sisters sprawled across the floor. They lay there lifelessly. Vinay must be twelve years old. He should have a job. "Where is Vinay?" she asked.

"He is gone." The old woman's wrinkled face puckered up, and she faked a sob. "I've done the best I can. Vinay is gone." Soup dripped into her hair as she scratched her head with a wooden spoon.

"Where is Rabindra?"

"He is dead. And Shanti is dead too," the old woman snapped. She could sense that her daughter despised her.

Kamola was incredulous. "What did they die of? Why didn't you tell me?"

"Child, I cannot go there. They do not give messages from the family."

"You managed to find me when you wanted to!"

"Yes, because we're desperate. I spent my last rupee to do it." She clanged a wooden spoon against the pot. "This is all the food we have, and your brothers and sisters are too weak to eat it!"

"How did they die? What happened?"

The old woman squatted on the ground and looked around the room. "I don't know. We woke up one morning and they were dead. Shanti choked to death. She had worms, you know?"

Kamola shuddered. "And where's father?"

"I don't know."

Kamola surveyed the room. "You sold the bed?"

The old woman looked at her daughter indifferently. "We have nothing."

"Why should I help you?" Kamola asked coolly.

The old woman shook her head. "I can think of no reason, child."

Kamola glanced at a corner of the room remembering what had happened there just three days after her twelfth birthday. Her father had been drunk, so she'd thought he wouldn't notice. But he had. Curiously he pulled her rags out of the corner and held them up. They were covered with Kamola's blood.

"Hey," he yelled. "Little Kamola is a woman." And he laughed while she cowered in shame. That night he raped her while three of her brothers and sisters sat ignorantly by.

"If you tell your mother, I will kill you," he'd said. Kamola could still feel his large hands gripping her like a vice. She could still see his sweaty body. She could often hear her own voice in her nightmares pleading, *Papa, don't. Please, Papa, don't.*

Kamola had wept silently at night. For three months, no one knew. Not a friend, not a sister. For three months she had kept her shame to herself, careful to please her father, but avoiding him desperately. Then one morning her mother had drawn her out. She collapsed in her mother's arms and sobbed. Her mother said she would help her.

And so at twelve years of age, Kamola was sold into prostitution. For two years she slept under the bed of Romesh Mondol, who taught her the art of pleasing men.

On two occasions Kamola had almost died. Once she had fled the large rambling warehouse where Romesh kept his girls. She could not make it on the streets. After three nights she returned. She was beaten severely, then left in the corner of a room with several broken ribs.

At another time, Kamola was overcome with great depression. She went to Romesh to beg him to help her find another way to work. "I will repay you everything, all the clothes and food you have given me."

Romesh laughed at her. "Kamola, you could not find a job that pays enough. You could work your lifetime and not earn what you do in a single month now. You are destined for this life. You are a natural. You are as fine as any of the girls I have ever known, and I am an authority on such things."

Kamola's depression increased. She could not eat. She became very sick. Romesh thought she would die. In desperation, Kamola made herself a pledge—since this was the life ordained for her, she would adjust to it as completely as possible. After this concession, Kamola's strength returned.

Her mother stared at her curiously. "I imagine there are a lot of things you could tell me."

"A lot has happened, Mama."

"Do you have friends?"

"I have friends."

"Have you been in love?"

Kamola stared out the open doorway of the tin hut. "Once," she said softly, "I was in love."

Her mother grunted.

"He was from Singapore. Have you ever heard of Singapore, Mama?" Kamola stared at her with amusement.

"Of course, of course," the old woman said.

"Do you know where it is?"

The old woman considered lying, but contempt made even the effort to impress too much trouble. "No, child, where is it?"

"It is hundreds of miles east of here. And I have been there Mama—on a jet plane."

The old woman stirred the soup. "What happened to this man?"

"He lied to me; he was married to someone else."

The old woman jumped, cackled with laughter, and beat the air with her wooden spoon. "That is a man. Yes, that is a man all right. Your old mama knows about men."

"Where did you learn so much about men?"

The old woman eyed her. "Well, you could teach me a few things." Then mustering all the seriousness she could, she limped over to Kamola and squatted next to her.

"Kamola," she spoke barely above a whisper. "We are dying. Look at the little ones. Can you help us?"

"What can I do, Mama? I cannot run away."

"You can!" The old woman snapped. "That's exactly what you can do! Molina Dasi did. She works for herself now and makes many rupees."

Kamola stared at her, astonishment mixed with horror. She was shrewd, this old woman in rags. She might not know Singapore from Bombay, but she was shrewd.

"I have thought of it, Mama. I am old enough now, but Romesh scares me."

"Romesh Mondol is an old man. Just a skinny old man. You were only a child when he bought you. It is not legal. He cannot do anything." The old woman smiled her toothless smile and twisted her fingers in her greasy rags, obviously pleased with herself.

"I would stay with you, I suppose?"

"No, child, you will have your own place. You are much too rich to stay here." The old woman knelt before her daughter like a beggar. "Just help the children from time to time. The little ones are so hungry," she whined.

"Mama, you have been so selfish and so foolish."

The old woman dropped her head. Kamola knew she felt no shame, but only acted a part in order to get what she wanted.

Kamola had hoped that childhood impressions of the old woman were incorrect. Kamola was confused. Her mother could not be an evil genius or she would not still live in such poverty, but the old woman certainly exhibited an uncanny shrewdness that brought back memories. She wanted to survive. Above all else she wanted to survive, and sometimes she made up for ignorance by dedication to that purpose.

"Mama, could I get some other kind of job?"

The old woman screeched in impatience. "Who is foolish, child? You are foolish. Your life is in the hands of the gods. They have decided what you are, and who is to say your kind of life is not much better than mine?"

"Perhaps. But where could I stay?"

Turning abruptly from Kamola, the old woman tugged at one of the listless children on the floor. "Get up. Get up!" Kamola's little brother sat up. His eyes glassy and dazed, he showed no sign of recognition.

"Run to Mrs. Samanta. Tell her your mama is coming. Can you hear me? Go!"

Kamola's mother turned and smiled. She was chuckling to herself. "This will work out. I have it all arranged. You shall see."

The little boy propped himself up against the wall, and slid slowly toward the doorway. Kamola wondered if he could support himself, let alone fulfill his errand.

"Off with you!" the old woman screamed. The little boy fell, picked himself up and scampered away.

"He is sick, Mama."

"Of course he is sick! We are all sick! Look at your brothers and sisters. We need the money. We are starving. Only you can help. I am sure." Kamola was silent. "You want out of this work? Mrs. Samanta will help you out. She is a Christian, and Christians believe in generosity. She will find a good Christian man who is wealthy."

The old woman frowned as if she suddenly feared that such a thing could happen. Then dropping her wooden spoon on the dirt floor, she limped out the open doorway.

Kamola glanced once more to that corner of the room, sensed the evil spirits lingering there, and hurriedly followed her.

Mrs. Samanta was very clean. Kamola could sense that, even though it was dark. They moved into the small room and squatted on the floor. "Come in, Mrs. Bala. This must be your daughter."

"This is Kamola."

"Your mother has told me all about you. You are welcome here."

Kamola felt a rush of excitement. Why not run away from Romesh? Why not live her own life? Mrs. Samanta's kind face gave her hope. This room would be as comfortable as the plywood box of a room at the warehouse. Romesh would not come looking here. She could work the streets freely. Kamola's arms tingled at the thought of freedom. She would make a fortune in weeks.

"Oh, Mrs. Samanta, can you help me?"

Kamola's mother was surprised and pleased with her daughter's performance.

"I will help you all that I can. My husband left me years ago. There is only myself and the children. We cannot do much for you, but you can live with us until these people quit searching for you."

Mrs. Samanta, sensing the desperation in the girl's voice, continued, "There's more, Kamola. The pastor of our church is a very great man. He helps many, many people. He has great power with God. If you really want help and if you are patient, he can arrange almost anything."

Kamola's mother could sense between Mrs. Samanta and her daughter a communication which she did not understand or like, but still things were working out. She crawled over to the woman, "Oh, Mrs. Samanta, thank you for having pity. Talk to that man about my children. He is very rich. He can help us."

Kamola, despising her mother's insincerity, knew that Mrs. Samanta could see through the selfish old woman and wondered why she offered to help.

"Mama, I will stay, and I will help the children. But you must never come here, or they will find me. Go quickly. I will bring you some money tomorrow."

As the old woman left, she paused at the doorway and turned slowly, "Mrs. Samanta, the gods will bless you. Kamola will reward you, too. She is very popular. We will make you a very rich woman." Laughing to herself, the old woman disappeared into the night.

"I do not want any money," Mrs. Samanta called after her. But Kamola's mother could not hear. She would not have understood anyway.

# 15

There is a room behind the large sanctuary on Royd Street. In the evenings people come there to pray. Sometimes the prayers are intense, as though the Christians wrestled with Satan himself. Sometimes they do.

The sahib spotted Kamola kneeling at a folding chair, her long hair almost touching the floor behind her. The sahib's wife caught his arm. "Kamola wants to give her life to Christ," she said.

The white man just stared at the scene. Several ladies from the church were praying next to Kamola. He had sometimes wondered if his sermons were penetrating the ears of the young Indian girl. A couple of teen-age boys stopped by the door and glanced in. Wherever you found Kamola there were several boys nearby.

"Go on, get out of here. Kamola is busy," the white man whispered angrily. He felt protective of the young Indian girl. He and his wife had spent many hours in prayer for her. He was keenly conscious of the tragic events which had brought Kamola to this decision. He wanted her to have every chance, for he knew that her conversion might come hard.

"How long has she been praying?" he asked.

"As soon as you finished your sermon, she came back here."

They crossed the room and sat down near the girl. "Kamola, they tell me that you want to become a Christian."

The Indian was aglow. "Oh, pastor, I am ready."

"You know what this means?"

"Yes, I understand, and I am ready."

He could catch the joy in her eyes. He took her hand and sighed deeply. There was much to do. In his office a man was waiting, a respectable man whom the pastor had promised to help find a job.

118

Then, there was 6,000 dollars that must come in that very month. His mind had been preoccupied by that all day. The money must come in soon, or the food program would have to be readjusted to meet increased prices. It would be a disaster for the children, already so malnourished that they sometimes fainted while waiting for their bread.

He patted Kamola's hand. All the frustrations vanished. This white man believed in his God. A new convert was the greatest joy he ever experienced.

Food, medicine and education he gave freely, but behind all was the hope that hundreds would receive his God, too. That sounded outrageous to some, who believed he was forcing western culture on the East. The white man was oblivious to such arguments. Passing out Jesus was as vital as passing out water to a man dying of thirst.

"Pastor, I want to thank you for giving me the job. I am so happy."

"Now Kamola, you understand that you do not have to become a Christian to please us. We are your friends anyway. We will always help you here."

"Yes, yes, pastor. Don't worry. I know what it is all about. I have been listening every day in chapel. I have decided I want Jesus. Many times I have wanted to come to pray, but I have always felt I could not."

"Kamola, Jesus died for you. He loves you very much."

The young Indian began to cry. She dropped her head in shame. She spoke very softly so that her voice would not carry. "Do you remember when you told me the story of the prostitute in the Bible? I will never forget that."

The pastor patted her hand gently. "Neither do I condemn you; go your way; from now on sin no more." Kamola wept. "You understand what this means?" the pastor asked. "This means that you cannot go back to your old life." Kamola nodded. "No matter what happens to your brothers and sisters, you must give your life to Christ. You cannot feed them all on the one rupee a day that we give you. We will have to find another way to help them."

"Pastor," she said. "I have not worked the streets since I talked to you and your wife. I have listened to all you have said, and I want Jesus in my heart. That is what you say to the children. That is what I want, Jesus in my heart."

"Kamola, Jesus will never refuse anyone. He loves you very much. He will come into your heart the minute you ask him. You know what you must do?"

The young Indian nodded her head. She stared for a long time at the floor, then deliberately lifted her head and spoke clearly. "Oh, God, I forgive my papa for what he did to me. It is all over. I forgive him." She burst into sobs. "I forgive you, Daddy. I forgive you." Kamola held on to the woman next to her, and they sobbed together, "Oh, God, forgive my mama too. She is very bad." Kamola prayed. "Mama, I forgive you."

"Now Jesus will forgive you," the white man said.

Kamola held her hands toward the ceiling, as the white man taught his people to pray. "Forgive me, Jesus. Forgive me of all the terrible things I have done."

"And Jesus is forgiving you, right now, Kamola. Jesus is in your heart right now. You are clean. Your sins are gone."


Kamola hesitated at the door of her mother's shack. She thought about not entering at all, but it was too late. The old woman had spotted her.

"Christian, Christian," she sneered.

*Mother must have talked to Mrs. Samanta,* Kamola thought. She stepped into the room.

The old woman was crouching over one of the little children, picking and cleaning the sores. The little boy lay inert, as oblivious to his mother's work as to the flies that clung to him.

"Christian," the old woman hissed.

Kamola could feel the anger and hatred in her mother's voice.

"Mama, they have given me a job with the children at the mission. Mama, I will still help you."

The old woman ignored her. Kamola had never worked the streets as thoroughly as she could have. She had been afraid of Romesh Mondol showing up. There had been very little money, but it had been enough to feed the whole brood of children. All that had stopped one week ago. There was no warning. There was no explanation. Suddenly the money had stopped coming. Mrs. Bala had learned what had happened. She knew all about Kamola. She knew all about her rupee-a-day-job at the mission.

The old woman lifted the little boy into the air by his leg, as if he were a chicken. She flopped the boy on his stomach and continued her work, this time on his back. Kamola recoiled at the sight of the little boy's back full of sores. She often felt guilty about the children. The old woman knew that, but strangely she was in no mood to torment Kamola. She covered the little boy's back with a rag; the flies stirred and then resettled.

"Mama, I will not go back to the streets."

"Child," the old woman spoke as though she were hurt and had been misunderstood. "No one ever asked you to live that kind of life forever. We just wanted your help for awhile. Your brother is dying." She paused and looked absently at the other children laying about. "They are all sick. I can hardly work anymore."

The old woman's face contorted. She sobbed, tears rolled down her face. The old woman just sat before Kamola sobbing.

Kamola was stunned by the scene. It was unlikely the old woman could have contrived such an emotional outburst. Kamola was surprised to see such feeling behind her mother's deceitful personality.

"Mama, Jesus doesn't want me to let you die. I know that. Christians are very generous, mama."

The old woman was clearly shamed for breaking down in front of her daughter. She returned to her sarcasm to save face. "If they are so generous, why do they pay you only a rupee a day?" she sneered.

"Mama, they do not really need me there. They are just kind. They are going to help me find a good job, then I will be able to help you."

"You cannot help anyone!" The old woman screeched. "You earn a rupee a day. Who are you going to help?"

"I will not let the children starve. I will go back to the streets before I will let that happen."

"You may already be too late for that. This one will not live." Kamola turned away. "Oh, he will die," the old woman insisted, "just as sure as Rabindra and Shanti died. He will die." She was hysterical now. "Leave us! Get out! You never wanted to help us. You are like your selfish father. You will run away again. You do not care about the children. Get out of here! Let us alone."

Kamola squatted next to her mother and waited almost five minutes in silence.

"Mama, some men from the United States are here," she said, trying to change the subject. "They are writing a book about the mission.

One of them, a Catholic priest, talked to me all day yesterday. They want to come here to talk to you."

The old woman only sniffed. "What do they want? Do they want to take pictures of the dying?"

"No, Mama, they are writing a story. They will ask you to remember things that you have said and done."

The old woman's face broke into its wide toothless smile. Kamola could not restrain laughter at her mother's expression. The old woman laughed too. "They should write about me," she said, turning to her daughter. "Your mother is a very clever woman. Very clever." She squinted her eyes, and for a moment Kamola imagined that the old woman was about to reveal some complex and evil thing she had done. Instead Mrs. Bala resisted the temptation and kept her thoughts to herself. "Very clever," she said again. "You would be surprised."

"Mama, they want to write about how I came to the mission, and about Christianity."

The old woman thought for a long time. "Child, what will you say when they ask you about your brothers and sisters? What are you going to do tomorrow? Are you going to be a Christian, or are you going to the streets to save your little brother?"

Kamola did not answer. The old woman looked into her face very closely. The broad toothless smile returned for she was sure she knew the answer. Kamola would not go back to the mission; she would return to the streets. It isn't possible to change destiny.

"I don't know what to do, Mama. I am just not sure anymore."

The mission seemed far away, the night of tears and joy a fantasy. This was real: the shack, the children, the terror that came from that corner of the room. This was not fantasy. *The gods have decided. The Hindus are right. There is no real choice for me. I must wait for some future life, perhaps then I can become a Christian.*

# Roughhouse

# 16

Calcutta is a city of violence. Even her mythological origins reek of blood. Legend claims the cadaver of her patron saint, Kali, burst and was scattered throughout south Asia. Her sacred toes landed at Kaligat, a holy place in Calcutta. Years after infanticide was outlawed in the 1820's, fanatical mothers still sacrificed their newborns in honor of Kali.

In the nineteenth century Calcutta became the great port city of the worldwide opium trade. Savage oriental pirates dropped anchor off her shores waiting to catch British ships returning for another load.

In the 1940's while India anticipated her long awaited independence from Great Britain, Moslem and Hindu political factions maneuvered to be the ones to wrest every advantage for their people. In Calcutta this rivalry surfaced violently. Gangs roamed the streets one evening in August of 1946, beating to death those of the opposite religious or political party. It turned into a night of sadistic frenzy. Tens of thousands were injured, and more than six thousand dead bodies were found. Many of the victims were women and children. Skulls had been split open with hammers, bottles, shovels, and sometimes large rocks. It was five times the death toll of the six-year, Protestant-Catholic war in northern Ireland. It had all happened in one night.

The next day swarms of giant, disease-carrying vultures descended on the streets like black clouds. Some who remember say the ugly scavengers feasted until they were too fat to fly. The vultures are still there. The new, highly respected Calcutta police force has tamed the city, but it has not been able to erase the legend. Calcutta is still a city of darkness and foreboding. A city of exotic mystery and sudden death. It should come as no surprise that there are those who feel drawn to such dark legends.

Jim Mix was such a man, a death-defying cyclist with the Russian circus. He thrilled audiences with cycling stunts in the *Well of Death*.

The Russian circus attracts a peculiarly rough crowd of men in Calcutta, men to whom Mix owed his small measure of popularity. These men were often in a well of death of their own and could appreciate the difference between a trick and a man who was literally defying the odds against life.

Drunk and cursing, this portion of his Calcutta audience exhibited a sadistic streak. As his cycle roared around the sides of the wooden tank, these violent men would call out, "Faster, faster." Speed pushed the cycle nearer and nearer to the top where a sudden thrust of speed could hurl him over the walls to his death. Mix felt the audience leading him into feats beyond any limit he had thought possible. There was a breathless pause, then the audience would roar with approval. Often afterward Mix would curse his stupidity.

"I can smell death," Mix often said. "There is a smell that comes just before death. I have reached that moment many times."

When the Russian circus left Calcutta, Jim Mix stayed. He was impressed with his demanding audience, the whores were cheap, and so was the liquor.

Calcutta challenged him as no other city had. He returned to a previous occupation, boxing. But it was not the kind of boxing which has been popularized in the West. "Roughhouse" Mix fought barefisted which requires a unique talent of its own. A boxer has to learn how to open a cut with his knuckles. There is always a lot of blood in such a fight. Mix, with his white skin, showed the cuts and bruises which had always made him popular to the brown audiences of the South Pacific and India.

Roughhouse lived in an abandoned garage. In its original state it could barely accommodate a very small automobile. Now it was smaller, because part of the building had collapsed. The cracks had been filled by rocks, mud, and strips of wood nailed to one another in a haphazard fashion. The roof leaked badly, except for the carefully prepared places above the mattress. The leaks formed little puddles on the dirt floor. When the rains were heavy these puddles overflowed and streamed into a ditch which ran like a highway

*Street people depend on public wells and pumps for all their water.*

through the middle of the floor. Rats sometimes raced along this highway. But Mix felt no need to dam it up. He could urinate and defecate in the trench. "I have my own toilet," he would boast. Needless to say, such luxury meant he had to live with the disease and smells accompanying the impromptu setup. Roughhouse was willing to pay the price; he was not known to be particular about his environment.

The mattress, however, did occasionally trouble Mix. It was stained with blood, urine and vomit. When it began to bother him, he would flip it over, preferring to sleep with the bugs and the cold dirt on the other side.

Mix reveled in the Calcutta night life. The city is not large in terms of space, but its bulging population of millions affords many combinations of entertainment. Roughhouse was on a perpetual drinking binge, conspiring with itinerant sailors to plan nights of pleasure. There were many fights, most of them drunken brawls outside of the ring. Though Roughhouse lived for years in Calcutta, he never exhausted its whores. Sometimes he ventured far from the docks in search of new opium dens. Sometimes he would explore crowded bustees where he would find someone desperate for money and willing to join one of his schemes.

One night, quite by accident, he wandered into a church on Royd Street.

The music, guitars and accordions lured him into the large auditorium. In his ignorance he only gradually concluded that it was a church. When the worship ended, a line of inquirers walked to the front. Remarkably, Roughhouse Mix, with a liquor bottle stuck in his back pocket, joined them.

Even now Mix does not know the reason for his actions that night. "It was providence," he says. Whatever the reason, Mix was soon under the spell of the white man, grasping hungrily for spiritual knowledge and considering carefully the pastor's warnings.

One rainy night, a few days after this, an old friend pounded on his door. She was a prostitute. The pastor had said to stay away from the prostitutes. "Go!" Roughhouse shouted furiously from inside his hut. But the pounding did not stop.

Mix was not one to trifle with, so he was surprised at her boldness. "You can pound all you want as far as I am concerned, I will not let you in," he shouted, deciding against roughing her up as then he might be tempted to sleep with her.

Rain flooded the street and gutters. The prostitute slumped by Mix's door. "Oh, please, Mr. Roughhouse," she said. "Please help me. Just let me sleep inside." She was crying.

Mix sat up on his mattress, annoyed and frustrated by her sobs. He was confused about what Christianity would say was right or wrong in a moment like this. He switched on the light, a single, low-watt bulb which hung from a cord that was threaded through the boards of the low ceiling, and poured himself a glass of cheap liquor. Then he sat back down on his mattress and listened to the girl sobbing outside. What was a Christian supposed to do? Finally Mix opened the door. "Don't try nothing," he said.

The girl stumbled in. She looked at Mix with a puzzled expression on her face, then she slumped to the floor.

Mix turned out the light and lay down. "Somebody beat you up pretty bad?" he asked. She did not respond. "Who would do that?" Roughhouse asked himself aloud.

The girl groaned. Mix waited to see if she was going to answer his question. When she did not, he grunted, rolled over on his mattress and went to sleep.

# 17

When the sahib returned to his office, his secretary called him immediately. "That man who came to church Sunday night telephoned this morning. He is in real trouble. He killed somebody last night."

"What?" The white man looked up from his desk.

"I didn't take the telephone call. Bimal got it."

"What happened? Was it an accident?"

"It was murder," she replied calmly.

"Oh, Lord Jesus. Oh, Lord," the pastor groaned, putting his head in his hands. "Is Bimal here?"

"Yes, he's upstairs."

The white man grabbed the telephone. "Bimal, what did that man have to say?"

"He took in some prostitute last night. Claims she was beaten up pretty badly and needed a place to stay. This morning he woke up, and she was dead."

"What did you tell him to do?" the pastor asked.

"Well, you weren't here. We didn't know what to do."

"Yes, yes, but what did you tell him to do?"

"We told him to call the police."

"Of course," the pastor said. "That is best. He should call the police."

"And they have booked him for first degree murder," Bimal added.

"But he did not do it, did he?" the white man asked excitedly.

"All we have is his story. He said he didn't do it."

The pastor shifted in his chair. "He said he did not do it," the pastor repeated loudly so that the secretary would hear him.

"Well, Pastor, we don't even know who this man is," Bimal said. "What was he doing with a prostitute in the first place?"

"Of course we know who he is. Of course we know who he is! He is our very own brother," the pastor explained. "He came to Jesus Sunday night."

"Well, yes," Bimal answered, declining to reason further. "What should we do?"

"I don't understand first degree murder," the pastor mused. "Why first degree?"

"He knew who this prostitute was," Bimal answered. "They were not strangers."

"Here is what we must do," the pastor sounded decided. "We will hear what he has to say, then we will hear what the police have to say. We will not jump to conclusions."

"Do you want me to go with you, my pastor?" Bimal asked.

"No, you have so much to do, I will handle this."

Roughhouse Mix had been thrown into a cell at the police station. It was packed, some inmates had been in for weeks. They leaned against the walls, sleeping on their feet, too lifeless even to fight over the extra food rations occasionally slipped to them by sympathetic policemen.

Somehow Mix had avoided a fight. The cell was too crowded even to lie down. Roughhouse did not expect his patience would last. Yet he had to try. He had heard many stories of the prisons in India. It would take great determination to survive even a couple of years. That is, if they did not execute him.

The white man arrived at the police station full of expectation. He knew many things about the Calcutta police. In spite of Calcutta's past legend as a haven for pirates and violence, her modern police force enjoyed a spotless reputation. It was efficient in its own spontaneous way, and compared to any other agency, remarkably free of corruption.

"I understand you have a man here by the name of Jim Mix," the pastor said.

"Just a minute," the young police officer looked agitated. He retreated to another room. A moment later he appeared at the doorway, "Would you step in here, please?"

The white man entered an adjacent room. In it was an old desk with piles and piles of papers and manila envelopes. There were many chairs in the room, almost all of them filled with stacks of dusty files. A ceiling fan turned slowly above them.

"Sit here, please," a policeman said sternly.

Several police inspectors were gathered around the old desk. One of them was a very young man with thick glasses. He had a pencil and notebook ready. "Now, you are here about Jim Mix. Is that right?"

"Yes," the pastor began eagerly, but he was interrupted.

"You have some evidence for us?"

"I am his pastor," the white man blurted out. "He has just begun to attend my church." The inspectors looked at each other. "What is he charged with?" the pastor asked.

"First degree murder," one of them snapped.

"Has he confessed to this crime?"

"How long have you known Mix?" the young man with the thick glasses said, ignoring the white man's question.

"Listen, inspector," the white man implored. "Several days ago this tough man came to my church. He gave his life to God. He has been willing to do whatever we tell him. I told him to quit smoking, and he threw his cigarettes away. He does whatever we say. He is willing to try whatever we suggest. It is a remarkable thing, but he just suddenly has faith in God."

"Now, sir, we don't dispute what you say," one of the officers said, "but this old man has a police record. He is known as a fighter. He has a reputation. We found the body in his place!"

"But didn't he come and report it to you?" the white man asked. "Didn't he tell you what happened? Why would he come to you, if he were guilty?"

"There wasn't anything else he could do," an old policeman said. He was standing in the corner of the room, smoking a cigarette and searching through a stack of files.

The young inspector picked up this line of thought. "What could he do, drag the girl to another place? Of course his only chance was to come and tell us his story."

"But we are the ones who told him to come to you," the white man said. "He contacted our church. We told him to report to the police. He does whatever we tell him. He is trying so hard to do what is right." There was a pause.

"What if you are wrong? What if he is innocent? What if one of these girls did come to him for help? What if someone had beaten her and he took her in? What a horrible injustice, to help her and then be thrown into prison for it. Oh, gentlemen, that would be terrible."

"All right, all right," the inspector waved his hands in the air. "Nobody said we had turned this over to the prosecutors yet. We will investigate his story."

"Reverend," the man in the corner spoke again, "those cells in the other room are packed with street vendors who were picked up for illegally selling liquor or for selling spoiled fruit. When we get someone for murder, we don't just let him go."

"But what was his motive?" the white man asked. "Why would he do it?"

"Those men don't need motives," the young one retorted. "They beat up girls for the thrill of it."

"We would probably have to go to second degree murder," the old inspector in the corner said.

"No!" the young one shouted. "No, we won't!"

The old policeman took a puff from his cigarette and gave the young man an icy stare. He picked up another stack of files from the nearby chair before he began to talk again. "I will promise you this, sir, we will give you a day. We will not turn anything over to the prosecutor until Thursday morning. I know you. You have been in here before about drug addicts. You are a good man." He took a long drag on his cigarette. "If I remember correctly, we even owe you a favor or two. We will promise you that much."

"Thank you," the white man was effusive. "Thank you. God bless you. This is the man's last chance. God wants to save him. You have saved a life."

The young policeman stood to open a door to another room. "I want you to talk to him yourself!"

"Thank you. I want to talk to him. You will not regret this."

The white man rushed quickly into an interrogation room. Three large cells opened off of it. Dozens of faces crowded against the bars. It was dark. It smelled horrible. The pastor waited patiently as they brought out Mix, who looked tired and weak. He was trembling. He sat on a stool across the table from the pastor.

"Oh, Jim, Jim." The pastor took the man's hand gently. "Jim, Jim," the white man now was shaking his head, "we are really in trouble." Roughhouse Mix sat silent. "Oh, God," the pastor prayed. "Give us Your strength, God."

Mix glanced around at the faces staring at him from behind the bars. He looked at the white man whose eyes were shut tightly. Mix bowed his head reverently. "Jesus, Jesus," the white man prayed. "Give us Your wisdom. Give us Your widsom. Thank You for Your saving power."

Roughhouse began to fumble with his clothes. The sahib finally looked up. There were several moments of silence. "How did this happen to you, Jim?"

"Well, sir," he shrugged. "This whore, a friend, came by last night. She was crying, and she was beat up pretty bad. I didn't know what to do. I remembered all you told me. I haven't smoked any." The pastor smiled.

"I haven't had no woman, either," he continued. "But I couldn't let her keep on crying out there. I told her that she could sleep way over on her side." Roughhouse looked pleadingly into the pastor's face. "I just didn't know what to do."

"Jim, the police say you beat that girl."

"Sir, Roughhouse Mix does not beat on the whores." The man straightened up tall on the stool. "You ask around. I have beat on lots of people over the years if they is disrespectful to me. But not the whores." The pastor said nothing. "I knows there are some men who beat women. But you ask around. I have always been nice to the whores."

The white man grabbed the fighter's hand and began another prayer. "Oh, God, please help us. This man is a very, very evil man." Roughhouse Mix dropped his head in shame. "He has done many violent things, but he has come to You. You never turn people away, Jesus. You came to save sinners."

"Oh, Jim," the pastor said, his face was contorted in anguish, "Satan always does this. He tries to finish us off when we stand for what is right. He is very angry. You have stood tall for Jesus, and Satan is very angry."

"Well," the old fighter said weakly, "I am afraid he has finished me off. There is no way they will let me out of here."

"Jim," the pastor shot back. "The Bible says that when you become a Christian you have Jesus for a lawyer."

The old man swallowed and then whispered. "Sir, do you think you could baptize me in this room?"

The pastor smiled. "Jim, you became a Christian the night Jesus saved you. He is already your lawyer."

The man's eyes filled with tears. "I'm not scared," he said. "I never been scared of nobody. I never been scared of death; I'm not scared now." The old man looked puzzled. "Still, I want to get out of here. I want to prove to everybody I didn't do nothing wrong. A year ago I wouldn't have cared," Mix said with a confused look on his face.

"Jesus will never fail you," the white man replied. "Jesus will get us out of this mess."

"Sir, I want to thank you for coming here today. That was a good thing to do." He spoke as if didn't expect much to come from the white man's efforts.

"Oh, Jim," the pastor implored, "is there anybody who knows you? Any friends I can talk to who might help us?"

Mix stared at the damp floor. "Well, sir, I have lots of friends, but they're all the kind you meet when you drink. Then, you don't see 'em again. Now I have lots of that kind of friend, but I wouldn't know very many names. I told you about the circus I was with. They knowed me real well, but they are all gone. I guess you'll just have to ask around. Lots of people know about me."

The sahib stood. "Jim Mix, I am your friend, and so is Jesus. The Bible says that Jesus will never leave you, nor forsake you. He will always stay with you." The pastor extended his hand. The old fighter grabbed it.

*This man has to be the filthiest person I have ever met,* the pastor thought. *He may have committed every crime in the book. What can we do, God? Do we throw him back in the water like a small fish? Do we give up just because the odds are against him? This man may turn his back on You tomorrow, God. Do you want me to believe him?* The white man knew what the answer was. He marveled at the love of God.

# 18

The Park Street police station assigned the Mix case to the young inspector. Friday morning he agreed to a meeting with the pastor from Royd Street. The white man arrived without the evidence he had hoped to find, but he had one desperate suggestion to make.

The policeman squinted through the thick-lensed wire glasses and smiled at the naivete of the white man. "Now, Reverend, why should we let this man go?"

"Because he is innocent."

"We don't know that," the policeman shifted in his chair. "This man will be convicted without a doubt. If the jury finds this man guilty, he is guilty. That's the way the system works."

"No," the white man said, shaking his head. "That man is only guilty if he committed the murder. If he did not do it, then he is not guilty no matter what you say will happen in a courtroom."

"Just a minute, Reverend." The policeman was exasperated. "If a person we both know will probably be found guilty by a jury should really go free, then there isn't anybody who should be convicted."

The white man guessed that the policeman had picked up some of the same information he had. It was not hard evidence, or even evidence at all. It was just the reputation of Jim Mix—nobody believed he had murdered the prostitute, not even the other girls. He wasn't like that. She had been seen with other men that night. No one had seen her with Jim Mix.

There was a pause. Not a long pause, but just enough for the white man to know that he was right—the policeman did not believe in Jim's guilt either.

"Do you know what it is like to be alone in the world?" the white man asked. "I mean absolutely alone. To have no son or daughter to fight for you? To have no neighbor who can vouch for you? Not even to have a personal friend?" The pastor pointed toward the interrogation room and the cell blocks. "That man in there doesn't even know who his parents are."

The inspector wore a pair of thick wire spectacles which he now removed and clutched in his right hand. "Reverend, that man is a circus bum. He has been around for years. He is not innocent. He has you believing all kinds of things."

"I know about people," the pastor protested. "All day long I work with people. I work with drug addicts, with orphans, with thieves—and I believe that man."

"He is a street fighter," the policeman shouted. "He is a drunk. He is probably the filthiest smelling man I have ever met." The inspector stood as if to emphasize the point. "He came into this station smelling worse than the men that have been crammed together in that cell for days without a toilet!"

"I have never met a man who could not change," the pastor said defiantly.

"Sir," the policeman gave a nervous laugh, "even he understands and accepts this. Who knows? Perhaps he has murdered others in his fights, and justice is only catching up with him. He does not blame us." The policeman pointed his finger at the white man. "You, you are the only one who does not accept this."

"Oh, no," the pastor pleaded, "please do not think that I am blaming you. I am not blaming you. I have the highest regard for this police department, and for you."

The inspector sat down. He ran his fingers through his hair.

"If you had the authority," the white man asked, "if you had the authority, would you let this man go?"

The inspector paused. He shook his wire glasses in the air as though they were an antenna which could pick up the answer. "Yes," he finally said. "Yes. I do not believe he murdered that girl." He paused as if he were not sure that he should say any more. The white man was leaning across the desk waiting anxiously for the policeman's next words.

"None of the other inspectors believes it either," the policeman said. The white man was silent for fear he would break the spell. "But he must be prosecuted. Even he has accepted this. He has committed many crimes!"

The white man closed his eyes tightly as if to pray. "But that is because he doesn't think that there is any chance. He has no one. He has no hope. He has changed, I tell you; he is not a criminal. He has changed. I have never seen a man whom God could not change."

The inspector leaped to his feet and waved his glasses. "Don't talk to me about God! Don't tell me that you speak for God!"

"I am not talking about God," the white man pleaded. "I am talking about a man's life. I beg you for this life. Give me this man's life. Please! Have mercy on this innocent man. He has changed. I will take all responsibility."

They were both sweating. The inspector took a handkerchief from his pocket and mopped the great drops of sweat from his face and neck. He walked to a nearby chair, picked up a folder and returned to his desk. The white man prayed silently. The inspector sat down. He took his glasses and wrapped the wire temples around his ears. The inspector studied the papers on his desk, and then began writing. "I'll tell you what I'm going to do, sir."

The pastor moved to the edge of his seat.

"I'm going to release this man. I am going to hold you responsible for him. I am going to parole him to you for life." The inspector looked up. "You have that big place on Royd Street?"

"Yes," the white man answered.

"He must never leave the grounds. The day he leaves the grounds we will arrest him, and we will never give him another chance."

The sahib was overwhelmed. He wanted to celebrate, but he held back. The inspector stared at him in bewilderment. "I have never met anyone like you in all my life." The white man was silent. The inspector continued to stare at him. "Why are you like this?" he asked.

The white man groaned. He thought of the long line of people waiting for him back at the mission compound. "There is so much pain. There are so many who need help."

"Who are you?" the inspector asked. "Who are you? Why do you assume all of this?"

"I am a servant of Jesus Christ," the pastor said boldly. "I am a servant, a lowly servant."

The inspector again laughed nervously. He shook his head in bewilderment.

"Today," the sahib added, "I am the happiest person in Calcutta."

"Well, if it gives you any peace of mind to have that man," the inspector said, "you can have him."

"You are a very fine person," the white man said. "God will bless you for this. You will never forget this day. God will show mercy to you some time. You will not be disappointed; there will be no trouble. I will stay with him every minute; he will never leave the compound."

The inspector just shook his head and waved the man away. "Alright," he said. "Alright. We will bring him to you tomorrow."

Fifteen years later Jim Mix told us his story. "I sleep right here," he said, patting the wooden bench we were sitting on. "I pull that other bench over here, and I have a pillow, and that's all."

I looked at Roughhouse Mix a little skeptically.

He laughed. "This is it. Really." Then he spoke very seriously. "This is what I want. I want to live close to the pastor. I sleep right here in the courtyard, and I sort of police the grounds. There are church services every night, and we are up at 4 A.M. When it rains I pull the bench under the roof over there."

Another member of our research team exchanged glances with me. Jim Mix smelled horrible. It was common knowledge that the old man refused to bathe. It prompted another question. "Are you still a faithful Christian?"

"Oh, I'm a Christian all right. My duty is with the pastor. I'm to look after him and his church here. That doesn't mean I still do all the things they tell me. I'll never quit chewing beetle nut. No doctor will stop me!"

"And when the pastor dies, what happens then?"

Roughhouse Mix squinted his eyes. "I only got one wish, one prayer. I've never asked God for anything in fifteen years and I've been thankful to Him for everything. I don't mind sleeping on this bench. One prayer is all I got, so it seems like He should give it to me."

We leaned closer since it appeared he was going to whisper.

"I asked God to let me go before the pastor. I want to die here on this property, working for the man in that office."

"What if he does die first? Where would you go then?" we asked.

Roughhouse Mix just stared into space. "I don't know. I don't know what I'd do. But that will never happen. God would never let that happen."

*Mark*

# 19

The sahib entered his office. He felt wonderful. He always felt that way after preaching to his students. He loosened his tie, and slumped exhausted into his chair.

Suddenly the white man remembered his appointment. His wife would be waiting for him at their apartment. He looked at his watch and whistled.

Mark Buntain glanced longingly at the pile of correspondence on his desk. Being the pastor of a church in Calcutta, India, is a difficult job. When the church has more than a thousand members, operates a school and drug rehabilitation centers, feeds thousands of people and maintains a small hospital, it is an impossible job.

The pastor thought of visiting the hospital briefly before leaving. There was a little boy he had brought in this morning. Then he sighed and shook his head; he must keep his promise. The whole staff was to take an evening off. It had sounded good to him at the time, but now that the evening had actually come, Buntain was already regretting it.

"He is here, he is here, Aunty!" Lorrisa shrieked from her lookout post by the stairs.

Mark Buntain entered the room, caught the look of disappointment in his wife's face, and slumped in a large chair.

"Mark, you're an hour late, and you're soaked!"

"Huldah, I'm sorry."

"Listen, Mark, you promised. The whole staff are waiting to go to the Club."

Buntain only moaned. The swimming club was once the splendid playground of British rulers. It reminded one of a great banquet hall with silver and china covering the tables, with servants standing nearby, lacking only one thing, guests. Occasionally, members of Calcutta's European community still come by. They swim in the pool and sit in the sumptuous gardens, sipping iced tea or lemonade.

The Buntains had visited years ago, when church officials had worried about their emotional and physical health. They were urged to go. It was suggested as a diversion for them, an escape from the pressures.

In fact, their few visits were tormenting afternoons for the Buntains. They were afternoons which conjured up images of life in America and Canada. They would talk about their friends in the West and wonder silently what kind of life their daughter would have if she were with them in Calcutta.

They had become frustrating afternoons to Mark Buntain. Sometimes he felt great guilt. He feared his Indian friends would link him to some of the more elite members of Indian society, those who were not always sympathetic to the cries of the hungry. He worked hard, this man. He worked so hard that one afternoon of rest struck him as unforgivable. There were masses of people who needed him.

Many years ago the Buntains had abandoned their idea of getting away from the pressures. The beautiful lawns at the club made them uneasy; the streets of Calcutta were much more comfortable. The Buntains were only members of the club; they had never really "belonged" at all.

"Mark, I don't care about this," Huldah exclaimed. "You know that. I have lots of work to do. But Felicia should slow down, and so should the others. They are all exhausted. They are giving their lives."

"Why do I have to go?"

Huldah sat down. "Mark, don't you see? They all respect you. They all drive themselves like you. If you don't join them, they will feel that you disapprove or think that it is unspiritual."

"Goodness, I don't disapprove!" Mark answered. "Felicia needs rest, and so do the others. They should get away. We should require it."

"So hurry up," Huldah called. "Let's go. It's not too late."

"Huldah, Huldah, wait a minute. Let me explain. I have been given an appointment."

Mrs. Buntain was startled. She understood immediately. They

were attempting to lease land for the new hospital and chapel. This needed government permission. They had been trying for some time to make arrangements to present their case.

"They have given us only a month to prepare." Buntain put his head in his hands.

"How did they get in touch with you?"

He shrugged, "I just got a letter in today's mail."

"Did you ask for an appointment?"

"Yes, yes, I did," Buntain said. "We have a right to that land. We signed an agreement. We will just have to raise the hundred thousand dollars, that's all!" Mark and his wife were silent. It was going to take a lot of discipline to have faith for something so impossible.

"Mark, we've got to go," Huldah sighed. "We'll start to pray and work on it tonight."

"And Huldah, I picked up a boy this morning. You've got to see him. He looks like a skeleton. Oh, it will break your heart."

"Let's go to the hospital," Huldah said smiling. "We'll take our evening off next week."


It was dark outside. The low-watt light bulbs cast a soft yellow glow in the tiny rooms of the hospital.

Sheema lay on the white sheets. She was unconscious. Felicia, walking by, glanced through the curtains and saw Buntain standing in the tiny cubicle. He was leaning over Sheema and praying quietly.

"I'm afraid we were too late," Felicia said.

"Well, Jesus is never too late. Jesus can heal her, Felicia."

"Yes, I believe that. There have been many wonderful miracles in this room." She called it a room, even though its walls were only plywood dividers, and its door was a curtain.

"That's right." Buntain picked up Felicia's train of thought. "That's right. Many miracles in this very room. No one ever believed that little Somnath would live. Look at him now!"

Buntain laid his hands on the little girl's cold forehead. "Oh, God, in the name of Your Son Jesus, heal this little girl. She has no one but You, God. She has no father or mother." Buntain stopped in mid prayer and turned to the young German nurse. "Felicia, the old man told me to take her, 'Nobody wants her,' he said."

145

Then Buntain continued his prayer. "Oh, Jesus, Son of God, nobody wants this little girl." Felicia bowed her head reverently. "Jesus, You want her," Buntain cried. "Jesus, You love her. You died for her. She is all alone in the world, there is no one to fight for her. There is no one to have faith for her. There is no one to pray for her. Jesus, save her. Let her live, so that I can tell her about this night. Oh, Jesus, let her live!"

"Pastor." Felicia interrupted his prayer. He was always praying. His prayers often did not have formal beginnings or endings. To talk to him, one often had to interrupt a prayer. "Pastor, Dr. Chatterjee is here. He is examining the crippled boy you brought in this afternoon."

"That's wonderful. Where are they?" Buntain started for the curtains.

"We put a cot in the outer hallway by the stairs," Felicia said, walking in long strides to keep pace with Buntain. "We really shouldn't do this, you know. We are too crowded as it is."

"Yes, I'll be more careful."

Dr. Chatterjee was standing with his hands on his hips. "This boy will walk if he lives."

"That's wonderful," Buntain said. "I thought it was possible. I don't know why, but it just looked as though it could be corrected. Remember Raju?"

"It's a similar situation, infantile paralysis. But Raju was much stronger. This boy would have died in a few more days. If he survives this week and gains strength, we will be able to operate on his hips and legs."

"This week is critical?"

"Yes, that's right." The doctor added, "We will have to have Dr. Agarwal for this. I haven't the experience to handle it."

"Doctor, you don't know what you mean to us. In the country I came from, I am sorry to say, very few physicians or surgeons would help anybody without money."

"We each must do what we have to do," the Indian doctor said.

"Yes, that's right, doctor." Buntain patted the old surgeon's hands. Then he whirled and strode off.

Chatterjee chuckled at Felicia. "What's wrong with him?"

"Oh," Felicia turned to watch the pastor walking across the compound toward his office, "we have a little girl he brought in yesterday, and I'm afraid we are going to lose her. Typhoid."

The old surgeon grunted.

"Would you like to see her?"

Chatterjee walked with her through the narrow hall. "You people are going to have to learn not to become so personally involved. You are going to kill yourselves, and we need you around this neighborhood."

"Oh, doctor," Felicia was shaking. "Tell the rest of them that. We've been trying to do too much."

Chatterjee stopped and listened carefully, like a wise old counselor.

"He's going to his office now," Felicia said. "He will pray for hours, probably all night long. This worries Huldah to death. If this little girl dies, he will drive himself for weeks. He will refer to it for months. We can't keep doing this. Why, dozens of people are dying within blocks of here right now."

"I know, I know," the old surgeon said. He had worked with the white man off and on for a long time. At first, like the other doctors, he had laughed at Buntain's eccentric manners and religious views. But they had stopped laughing long ago. They loved him now, like the people.

"Well, I sound like the westerner now, but there is nothing admirable about driving yourself to death. He needs rest; all of you do. This is crazy."

Emotionally Felicia had been ready to break, but something the doctor had just said steadied her. "And you, doctor, how much rest do you get?"

Chatterjee just stood for a moment. They stared at each other. The old doctor shook his head.

# 20

At midnight the pastor's office was dark. Perhaps the sahib was not there after all. It would be highly unusual for him to be sitting alone in a dark office. Bimal glanced at two men talking nearby. He could hear the deep voice of one and identified it immediately as that of Roughhouse Mix.

"Where is the pastor?" Bimal called.

"He doesn't want to talk to anybody," the voice answered.

"Is he on the compound?" Bimal asked.

"He's around," Mix replied.

Bimal sighed. "Look, this is really important. I have to talk to him. Mrs. Buntain sent me here." Bimal pleaded.

Mark Buntain had asked to be left alone, an unusual request from him, so Mix had posted himself near the office to intercept the inevitable train of people needing to see the pastor. But Mix could feel the urgency in Bimal's voice, so he only shrugged his shoulders. "He's in there."

Bimal pounded on the door. "My pastor, let me in. Pastor. Pastor!"

Mark Buntain opened the door, but did not switch on the light.

The Indian groped for a seat and stared toward the desk, where he could just make out the outline of Buntain. "What's wrong, Pastor?"

There was a long silence.

"I'm just praying, Bimal. I'm just praying."

"About the land?"

"Yes."

"Well, we are all praying, Pastor. I am sorry about the little girl. I know how it hurts you."

"Yes, Bimal, it hurts very much. Satan is very deceptive, Bimal. He will tell us that we cannot have the hospital this year. We cannot believe him."

Buntain wanted to confide in his Indian friend. He wanted to pour out all of his frustrations and doubts. He wanted to tell Bimal how sometimes it seemed that all the prayer and work of twenty-three years had not made the slightest impact on Calcutta. For every orphan they had found, one hundred had taken their place on the streets. For every drug addict they had cured, hundreds had died. They had worked hard, they had given every waking minute to God, but the fact remained that the problems of Calcutta were now much, much greater than they had been twenty-three years ago. Buntain ached to talk about his fears that there would be no hospital. There was not enough money. The Indian government would never release land to them.

The Indian shifted uncomfortably. His eyes had adjusted to the room, and he could see Buntain staring at him. "Talk to him," Huldah had said. "You are his friend, Bimal. Ask him about his childhood. Ask him about his father. Get him talking about why he came to India." It was going to be awkward.

"Pastor, I've been wondering . . ."

"Yes, Bimal." Buntain was gentle.

"I have often wondered about God's will, pastor. How can I really know what He wants me to do?"

Buntain clasped his hands and prayed silently. *God, why doesn't he just tell me what his problem is? This terrible pride.* "Well, Bimal, I don't know how to describe it." Slowly, Buntain nibbled at the bait. "You will have assurance and peace. You will just know that it is God's will. But you must have faith too."

"You are always so sure about things, pastor. God talks to you so clearly. It is easy for you."

"Oh, Bimal, Bimal. I am no different than you. We all must come to God in faith."

"What if God has spoken to me, and I do not know? How did you know that you were supposed to come to India?"

Buntain frowned. "Oh, that is a long, long story." He watched the shadow of the ceiling fan turn slowly.

"Well, then," Bimal implored, "tell me how you knew you were supposed to be a minister."

The white man leaned back in his seat. He was a dear friend, this Indian. They had been through a lot together. What crisis could he be facing now? Why such urgency?

"I always knew I was supposed to preach," Buntain said. "I knew it when I was a little boy in Canada. I used to preach to the pillows in my house. I would stand them up and preach to them." They both laughed.

"You never doubted that you would be a minister?"

"Oh, I had doubts, sure. I almost went into radio. I loved radio." Buntain sat up in his chair. "You know how I get so excited when we have our Christmas pageant here?"

Bimal thought about the pastor's Christmas productions and smiled.

"I love that sort of thing," Buntain said, "I love drama. I loved radio; I used to stay awake all night listening to the announcers."

"But you didn't get a job?"

"Yes, I did."

"You were an announcer?" Bimal relaxed. It was working.

"I was a disc jockey. I wanted to know everything about broadcasting. I worked hard. But Bimal, I was so empty, so empty. I was so disappointed." Buntain paused.

"Then how did you become a pastor?" Bimal asked.

"I had a late disc jockey show one night. I left my boarding house and walked to the radio station. Our studio was on the fourth floor. I stepped into the elevator. Something happened.

"It's hard to explain, Bimal. A terrible spiritual conflict had been going on in my soul. When I stepped into the elevator I suddenly felt the glory of God leave my life. I could see it. It was like heat waves going down the hall away from me. I was cold all over. I knew that I had grieved the Lord."

Buntain stood and walked to the glass window at the door of his office. "I went to the studio. Normally, I was very calm and quiet, but I began to perspire all over. My heart was crying out. I finished my disc jockey show, did the night newscast for the British Air Press and walked out."

Buntain wiped the distorted windows of his door as though he could somehow clear the view. The light bulbs from the courtyard sparkled like diamonds in the tiny glass prisms of the windows.

*Mark Buntain chats with the author, Douglas Wead, on a Calcutta street.*

*An Indian medical worker treats one of Calcutta's many lepers.*

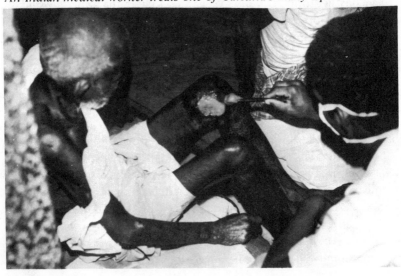

"I had to go through the grounds of the high school. I remember that it was a clear night; the stars were very bright. I was crying in my heart, asking God to help me." Buntain was far away now.

"When I got to my boarding house it was midnight. Mrs. Wilson had my supper ready for me. She was a Pentecostal Christian. How she prayed." Buntain paused. "I tried to eat, but I couldn't. Tears began to flow down my face.

"She said to me, 'Mark, what's wrong?'

"I said, 'I've got to get out of radio. God wants me to preach.'

"She threw up her hands and said, 'Oh, praise God. I've been praying for this.' "

The white man smiled and waited for a long time before continuing. Bimal sat patiently.

"Well, I didn't know anybody had been praying for me except my mother and father. They always prayed for me. I went into my room. At two in the morning I said, 'Jesus, if You will take this craving for the world from my heart, if You will take away this craving for money from me, I promise I will preach the gospel.' " The Indian saw a tear on the pastor's face.

"It left. Just like that, Bimal. It all left."

Buntain began to pace around the small office. "Oh, hallelujah. Thank You, Jesus. Praise You, Jesus. The glory of God came back."

The pastor stopped. "I always wanted to help the poor," he said. "I used to take some of my clothes to school and give them to the black children, even though we were very, very poor ourselves."

There was silence.

"Did your father want you to come to India?" Bimal asked.

"Oh, no," Buntain smiled. Then suddenly he whirled at Bimal. "Did I ever tell you about my father?"

"No." Bimal sat back in the shadows delighted and a little embarrassed by the honor of hearing such a story.

"My father was a very great man, Bimal. A great man. He was in charge of many churches in Canada. He was like a bishop over the whole country for the Assemblies of God. He built a great church and a college. He taught me everything. He always wanted me to take over his church and the school, but I wanted to be a missionary.

"When Huldah and I arrived in Calcutta, everything was in a mess. The missionaries that were here were locked in terrible disagreement.

The Indian church leaders didn't want us; the missionaries told us to go back. As though this were not enough, we were experiencing terrible cultural shock.

"Bimal, you can't imagine the staggering shock of a westerner's first trip to Calcutta. We moved into the apartment we are in now. That was twenty-three years ago."

The pastor returned to his desk. The Indian had heard how stunned westerners were at the poverty of Calcutta. He remembered his first day in the leper colony and wondered if it were like that, but concluded it could not be that serious.

"Was your father angry?" Bimal asked.

"Oh, no," Buntain answered. "Three days after we arrived, I received a cable from my mother. She said that Dad was dying of cancer and wanted to know if I could come home. So I left Huldah and the baby here, got on the plane and flew home." Buntain sat up.

"That's a remarkable example of God's power, Bimal. Do you know that I didn't have any money, so I just prayed. That very day I went to the BOAC counter and told the young man my story. I said, 'My father is dying. Your office says there is one ticket available, but I have no money. If you will help me, I am sure that when I get home I can send you the money for the ticket.'

"He said, 'I am a Christian. Don't worry. I will help you.'

"They must have phoned other missionaries in town to check me out, because without my having to sign my name to a paper, they gave me a first-class return ticket to Edmonton, Canada. They wrote across it, 'compassionate.' " Buntain shook his head as though he could not believe his own story.

Bimal encouraged him. "That's wonderful, Pastor."

"My brother, Fulton, met me at the airport and took me straight to the hospital. Dad was in precarious condition. The doctors had opened him up and found him full of cancer.

"I went to a women's missionary prayer meeting. The minute my knees hit the floor, God broke my heart for India." The pastor groaned, as though experiencing the sensation again. Buntain stood up. "Up to that time, I had no special call from God to come to India. I had left New York and gone to India, because it was my assignment. I had no desire to be here. None whatever. I didn't want to be here. But the moment I got on my knees, God broke my heart for this city.

153

For two hours I wept and cried for Calcutta." Buntain began to wring his hands.

"You love us, Pastor," Bimal said.

"Oh, how I love you. I love this place," the white man said. Tears began to roll down his cheeks. "I love Calcutta. This is the last hole this side of hell, but God has given me such a burden." Buntain sat back down. "Oh, thank You, Jesus, for calling me to Calcutta."

"Did your father ever accept your decision?" Bimal asked.

"Oh, yes. My father called me to his bedside and said, 'Mark, it's always been my desire to have you take over the work here in Canada—the church, the Bible school, everything—but as long as there is one man without Christ in India, you must go back.' "

Mark Buntain stood up, his face aglow. "Bimal, I turned around, left him, got on a plane, and flew back to India. How great is my God!" The white man began to pace around his tiny office. "Thank You, Jesus. Thank You for calling me to India. Thank You for counting me worthy to suffer with these people! Thank You, Jesus, for the hospital You are going to give us."

Bimal prayed softly. "Oh, God, You have given my pastor new strength and faith."

Buntain's shoulder accidentally brushed the wall, switching the ceiling fan to a higher speed. Stacks of letters and papers whirled into the air. Bimal snatched about him trying to catch the papers. Buntain turned the switch for the fan, then found the lights.

Instead of turning the fan off, he had switched it to its highest speed. Both men were momentarily blinded by the bright light. When they could see again the room was awhirl with paper. Buntain was reminded of a pillow fight with his brother Fulton, long ago in Canada. The room had been filled with thousands of tiny feathers.

The two men broke into hearty laughter as they chased the papers about the room. Buntain hurried frantically as though his father really might burst in at any moment, shouting, "Fulton and Mark, what have you done?"

When the room was finally restored to order, Bimal slipped out quietly.

Roughhouse Mix sat on the steps by the pastor's office. As the night passed he patiently scanned the dark courtyard and listened to the sounds coming from the street. A dog would bark. A drunk would shout. Occasionally he leaned back against the the door to listen to the pastor's prayers. "Thank You, Jesus. Thank You, Jesus!" the pastor would be saying. Mix's expression never changed.

The lights had been on in the office ever since Bimal had left. The white man's mood had clearly changed. Mix wondered what had been said, but he was perfectly content not to know.

There were several bags of cement stacked over near the shed that Mix was especially concerned about. One bag would bring Re. 20.00 on the black market. No doubt someone would try to steal them tonight. Mix wondered if the cement would ever be used. He wondered why so much was being bought when as yet they didn't have the land. He wondered if the pastor ever would build his hospital.

*We shall know soon about the land,* he said to himself. *We shall know within a month.*

# 21

Buntain waited nervously in the sitting room with his associate pastor, Ron Shaw. Buntain wondered if and when he should speak. He wondered if he might be able to say something that would be the key to the negotiations.

"Dr. Buntain?"

"Yes." He leaped up and walked to the receptionist's desk.

"I'm sorry to have kept you waiting for so many hours, but I was unable to get hold of Mr. Kundu's appointment secretary. He simply won't be able to see you. He will be leaving the city for two weeks and he has a full schedule."

"Well, Ma'am, we won't take a lot of his time. We have waited almost a month for this meeting. I have his correspondence right here. A lot of lives depend on this." *Easy does it,* Buntain thought. *Don't push too hard.* Inside he felt panicky.

"Yes, I understand. He gave me the name of a Mr. Mohan Mullick, a member of the legislature who will be able to meet with you this week. This might actually save a lot of time since Mr. Mullick has much more to say on these matters."

"Oh, no." Buntain bit his lip. "You see, we have met with Mr. Kundu. He knows who I am and is familiar with our work. We would have to start all over if we met with someone else."

The secretary began to give the first signs of impatience. "Yes, I understand, but I can do nothing."

Buntain resisted any more conversation. "Thank you for helping us."

Ron Shaw followed the pastor to the car. Buntain slumped over the steering wheel. "God is leading us, Ron. I have seen many miracles. I

156

can almost feel them before they come. Praise You, God. Thank You for the new hospital! Praise Your Name, Jesus!"

The young Indian said nothing. *We will not get the hospital this year,* he thought. He studied the pastor as they sped through the streets. *He is a great man. He will give his whole life for India, but they will not give him his hospital. He hopes for it, and he prays for it, but he will be buried here without seeing his hospital.*

Buntain parked the car and trotted briskly up the steps. Shaw did an occasional double step to keep pace. They wandered down several corridors and in and out of several offices before they found Mr. Mullick's.

"We wanted to make an appointment with Mr. Mohan Mullick," Buntain smiled at the secretary.

"I am sorry, he is very busy."

"Yes, we understand that. We don't expect to see him for several days." Buntain was bluffing for he did not know if a meeting could be arranged within a month's time. One never knew what to expect.

"Just a minute," the secretary said. Then before the two men had even looked around the room, she motioned to them. "You may go in."

Ron Shaw was momentarily startled. Buntain felt it was premature, but there was nothing he could do about it now. Mr. Mullick rose to greet his visitors. "Aha. So you are Dr. Buntain. This is a surprise."

Mark stared curiously, for he knew the man standing in front of him. A great fear swept over him as he realized that he could not remember when they had met. He did not want to insult this man he needed so badly.

"How is the little crippled boy?"

Buntain hesitated, "Raju?"

"Yes, Raju." Mullick laughed. Buntain smiled broadly. "I'm the man who was standing in the rain."

"Yes, yes, of course," Buntain said excitedly.

"I was waiting for a taxi, but you insisted on taking me home."

"Yes, I remember." Buntain felt suddenly warm; it was as though God were wrapping His arms around him.

"How is Raju?" Mullick asked again.

"He is fine, he's fine. I wish you could see him. He was operated on three times by one of the finest doctors in this city. He is walking."

Mullick's eyes glistened with tears. He studied Buntain. Ron Shaw looked helpless. Who was Mr. Mullick?

"We have so many needs," Buntain said. "Mr. Mullick, we need the hospital. Help us. Help us if you can. We only want whatever the government wants, but if you let us buy this land we will build a great hospital, and we will fill it with people like Raju."

No one spoke. Ron Shaw felt weak. Where had the pastor met this man? How did he know about Raju? Was this something God had arranged?

"Well, I don't think there will be any trouble. We will release this land for you." Mullick tapped some papers on his desk. "You have done very good work on Royd Street."

*Thank You God.* Buntain felt excitement bursting inside. *Thank You God. Help me to be calm.*

There followed an afternoon of detailed discussion about the planned hospital: its operation, its financing, and details about the neighborhood.

Buntain and Shaw, amazed, found themselves finally using papers and documents they had carried to many appointments. Past discussions had seldom advanced far enough for such details. Now they gladly produced letters and statistics to illustrate their plans.

When Buntain returned to the compound, he was exhausted. Somehow the word had rushed ahead of him; there were victory smiles on the faces of the workers.

When Huldah stopped by the office, it had begun to rain.

"Today seemed like a dream," Buntain said. "But I think we're going to get that land."

"It is no dream," Huldah assured him. "God is going to raise up a hospital."

The pastor sat at his desk. He leafed through a stack of letters. "It is going to be difficult," he said.

"Financially?" she asked. Buntain nodded. "Will Canada help us?"

"I wish I knew," the pastor replied. "We have correspondence and promises from government agencies in the various provinces."

"How much could we get?"

"Well, if they all do what they say, we could get as much as three hundred thousand dollars."

Huldah grimaced. "Oh, Mark, we are going to need much, much

more than that. We will have to raise hundreds and hundreds of thousands of dollars more than that."

The rain became a downpour, rattling noisily on the roof.

Buntain sighed. "Huldah, I don't want us to compromise any of our programs. The food distribution, the school, everything must go on as usual. We must not stop one thing."

She nodded. "We can borrow if we have to," she said. "You have a good reputation. There must be many institutions that can support this. They all respect you and trust you."

"We will get the money somehow, but it will mean a lot of work for everyone."

"Oh, Mark, God will give us the strength. He has not brought us this far to let us down."

"It will be quite a burden," Buntain said. "We will be assuming a debt of more than a million dollars. We have no guarantees, Huldah—I mean we may get a thousand dollars from one source and never hear from them again. They are not committed. It is all so unpredictable." He looked at her seriously, for he wanted her to know even more demands would be made on their time and privacy. Could she take any more?

She sat down, ignoring his question by asking one of her own. "What about the mission board?" she said. "Perhaps they will not approve."

Buntain grabbed his wife's hand. They were both silent.

"Oh, God," the white man prayed after awhile, "You have never failed us. We have always depended on You. You have called us to build this work. We have given our lives for this place. You will not fail us."

He squeezed his eyes tightly shut and shook his head. All the emotion of the day poured out of him. "Oh, Jesus, think of the children, the hundreds and hundreds of children. Let me live to carry some little child into that great, great hospital. What a day that would be! You would be given all the glory, Jesus. This is Your work."

Huldah patted her husband's hand. The strain of the last few weeks was showing on his face.

"Oh, God, don't let me die like Moses, without entering the promised land." Buntain collapsed in exhaustion. "Oh, God, help us build that place right away. Forgive me of any sin and have mercy on me. I will do whatever You want me to do, God."

The rain splashed on the glass door. Huldah did not wait for her husband to finish his prayer, but once more patted his hand, then stood and opened the door. The thick sheets of rain were washing the courtyard. Silently they watched it, each lost in a thought world of his own.

That summer work on the hospital began. While the land was being cleared a curious thing happened. An Indian worker came rushing across the grounds chattering with excitement. He had found the lost grave of William Makepeace Thackeray. Or so he said. It sounded far-fetched, but it was soon confirmed. He had indeed found Thackeray's grave.

The irony of that discovery was not lost on anyone. Thackeray, living in Calcutta, had become quite cynical toward God and man because of the suffering he witnessed. Now above his bones, was rising a testimony to the fact that God was at work even in this dark corner of the world. The white man seized on the event as the harbinger of miracles.

Financial miracles were what he had prayed for. Now that the day of his dream was upon him, he felt himself being crushed beneath the enormity of the project. Somewhere beyond the reach of his contacts, he must find an extra million dollars or more. Daily he sifted through the stacks of mail looking for sponsors. A letter to an old friend might bring twenty dollars, or it might bring a hundred. How many personal letters could he write and pray over in one day? God could give him a miracle even as He had some of the drug addicts who had experienced miraculous cures without withdrawal.

"You cannot tell me it is coincidental that Thackeray's grave has been found on our property," he told his wife that night. "God has planned this hospital for years. God loves this neighborhood. He has been watching us, and He has seen the suffering. God will raise up that hospital just as you said."

On Sunday, work on the hospital stopped. The pastor insisted on a traditional sabbath, which meant no work on Sunday. Roughhouse Mix stood silently by the gate of the compound, watching the worshipers fill the sanctuary.

"Hey, Mr. Mix," a young man called.

Jim turned to see Ram Dutta approaching. Ram worked in the

print shop. He had been trying to get to know Jim Mix, but the tough old man was difficult to talk to.

"Join me for a cup of tea." Ram nodded to the open tea stall across the street. "Please."

Roughhouse stared across the street as though it were another country. He hesitated, looked back toward the sanctuary, and then walked to the tea stall.

Ram Dutta and Jim Mix sat together in the stall. Ram had been wanting to talk to someone for a long time. He was beginning to miss his once luxurious life style. Ram did not know what kept Mix glued to the compound, but he knew Roughhouse had been all over the world. Perhaps he had a story similar to his own. The young Indian only knew that he had to talk with someone who understood, someone who knew about life beyond Calcutta.

Mix glanced nervously about and took a sip of tea. Suddenly he gasped for air. His face was turning white. Dutta stared at the old man in horror.

"Help!" Ram Dutta raced across the street and into the compound courtyard. "Help!"

Dwight Dobson was the first to reach the old man, who was by then lying on a bench in the tea stall. Dobson, a karate expert on loan to the Calcutta police, took charge; Jim Mix was carried across the street and into a small hospital cubicle.

No one dared interrupt when the white man was preaching, not even with such dramatic news. But when Mark Buntain finished his sermon he was rushed out of the sanctuary and into the hospital.

"It's Jim," Dobson said. "He's had a stroke."

Buntain hurried into the small cubicle. Nurses and members of the staff retreated from the room, pulling the curtain closed. "Jim," Buntain called. "Jim!" The muffled voice of the old man spoke then, very awkwardly and slowly. No one could hear except for the white man who was leaning close. Then silence.

The staff waited patiently outside the curtain. At last Buntain called, "Nurse." When the curtain was parted, Jim's head lay peacefully on Buntain's lap. His only prayer had been granted. Jim Mix had died first.

Mark Buntain left the hospital. He started to get into his car, then hesitated, remembering that Mix was not there to open the gate.

Slowly Buntain opened the gate himself, slipped into the front seat of his car and turned out onto Royd Street.

He sped through the crowded street, honking his horn frantically. His eyes were blinded by tears. When he neared a Muslim bustee he stopped, locked his car and walked briskly into the narrow alleyway. The people stared. Some followed him at a distance.

He had only walked a block when he saw Raju far ahead of him, a skinny little boy who walked awkwardly and slowly. The many people around him seemed to zoom past. Raju would lift his leg and swing it out and around. He moved forward with a slow, jerking movement, yet he walked with great pride. The white man was soon at his side.

"Pastor!" Raju exclaimed.

"I didn't get to visit your Sunday School class today," Buntain said, looking casually about at the squalor of the neighborhood as though out on an evening stroll. "I missed you, Raju."

"Are you coming to visit me?" the little boy asked. He did not really expect that the sahib had come just to visit him.

"Yes, I just wanted to see how you were doing," the white man answered, covering his grief.

"Oh, I am doing fine," Raju answered confidently. He walked as carefully and as smoothly as he could, and smiled proudly back at the many faces that followed them. He was honored to be with the pastor.

They found Asha, Raju's mother. She smiled and fumbled with her rags, not certain what to do. There was no chair to offer the white man, there was no food or drink. There wasn't even a roof, for they still lived against a mud wall near the Muslim man's shack.

Raju was not self-conscious. The white man sat down, leaning against the wall and stretching out his legs in the mud and the urine as though relaxing on a large couch. For a long time they sat arm in arm laughing and chattering about the school and teachers, yet Raju noticed that through it all the white man wept. From a short distance, the crowd watched the strange spectacle.

Buntain talked about God, and Raju answered back with his own Bible knowledge. Once the white man began to sing softly, an old tune from some distant part of his past. It was out of place in the Muslim slum. The people, crouched on their haunches, inched forward mesmerized by the atmosphere created by the sahib. They were like Hindus taking darshan, a spiritual experience which happens in the presence of a great man. "I'll go where you want me to go, dear Lord," the pastor sang, crying softly, "o'er mountain, o'er plain, o'er sea." Raju chimed in with his squeaky voice, humming when he couldn't pronounce the English words.

Mark Buntain glanced around at the dozens of faces watching him sing. He was unable to stop the flow of tears. Raju sang too, singing louder each time they repeated it. He was fearless in the arms of the white man even though it was a Muslim neighborhood, even though the strange sahib would leave, and he would stay.

It was getting dark and the bustee was no place for a white man to wander at night. In another hour he might not be able to get out.

*I just came to thank You, God.* Buntain prayed silently. *Jim Mix is free. He is free at last. I just wanted to thank You for sending the rain that day, and for Mr. Mullick, and for Raju, and for the land. I want to thank You for sending me here, Lord. I'm now ready to work for You, Lord. We'll get the help we need. We'll do it, one letter at a time.*

"Good night, Raju." Mark Buntain suddenly slapped his leg, there was work to do.

"Good night, Pastor."

"See you tomorrow," the white man said. Tears still glistened on his cheeks.

"Pastor?" Raju smiled broadly. "You are leaving, but Jesus stays with me all the time."

"Yes, He does. You are right."

"Right here is where He sleeps," Raju joked, expecting the white man to laugh as he had at his other jokes.

But the white man glanced at the pile of rags and at the slime dripping from his pants and said nothing.

Raju watched silently until Mark Buntain had disappeared down the long narrow alleyway.

(Further inquiries or contributions to the Calcutta Christian Mission Hospital may be sent to Calcutta Mission of Mercy, 1717 South Puget Sound, Tacoma, Washington 98405)